BAIL SERVICES IN SCOTLAND

Bail Services in Scotland

The Operation and Impact of Bail Information
and Accommodation Schemes

GILL McIVOR
SUE WARNER

Avebury

Aldershot • Brookfield USA • Hong Kong • Singapore • Sydney

Published by
Avebury
Ashgate Publishing Limited
Gower House
Croft Road
Aldershot
Hants GU11 3HR
England

Ashgate Publishing Company
Old Post Road
Brookfield
Vermont 05036
USA

British Library Cataloguing in Publication Data

McIvor, Gill
    Bail services in Scotland : the operation and impact of
    bail information and accommodation schemes. - (Evaluation
    studies in social work ; 5)
    1. Bail - Scotland 2. Criminals - services for - Scotland
    I. Title II. Warner, Sue
    364.9'411

    ISBN 1 85628 626 6

Library of Congress Catalog Card Number: 96-84018

Printed and bound by Athenaeum Press, Ltd.,
Gateshead, Tyne & Wear.

Contents

Tables

Series editor's preface

Evaluative Studies in Social Work brings together research which has explored the impact of social work services in a variety of contexts and from several perspectives. The vision of social work in this series is a broad one. It encompasses services in residential, fieldwork and community settings undertaken by workers with backgrounds in health and welfare. The volumes will therefore include studies of social work with families and children, with elderly people, people with mental and other health problems and with offenders.

This approach to social work is consistent with contemporary legislation in many countries, including Britain, in which social work has a key role in the assessment of need and in the delivery of personal social services, in health care and in criminal justice. It also continues a long tradition which perceives an integral relationship between social work, social research and social policy. Those who provide social work services are acquainted with the complexities of human need and with the achievements and shortcomings of major instruments of social policy. This knowledge was exploited by, amongst others, Booth, Rowntree and the Webbs in their studies of poverty. Politicians and sociologists have also recognised that, together with the people they try to help, social workers can provide a commentary on the human meaning of public policies and the social issues that grown from private troubles.

This knowledge and experience of the recipients and practitioners of social work is not, of course, immediately accessible to the wider community. A major purpose of research is to gather, organise and interpret this information and, in the studies in this series, to evaluate the impact of social work. Here there are many legitimate interests to consider. First and foremost are direct service users and those who care for them. These are the people who should be the main beneficiaries of social work services. Also to be considered are the personnel of other services for whom liaison and collaboration with social work is essential to their own successful functioning. The needs and views of these different groups may well conflict and it is the researcher's task to identify those tensions and describe social work's response to them.

The problems which confront social work are often extremely complex. They may need to be tackled in a variety of ways; for example, through practical assistance, advocacy, counselling and supervision. Outcomes may be similarly varied and studies of the effectiveness of social work must demonstrate the different kinds of impact it can have. These may entail changes in users' circumstances, behaviour or well being. On these changes, and on the kind of help they have received, users' perspectives must be of great significance. Also of central interest to those who provide or manage services is an understanding of their form and content and the relationship between the problems identified and the statutory responsibilities of social workers and the help given. Social work researchers must therefore take care to study what is actually delivered through social work and how, as well as its outcomes, aspirations and objectives. For good and ill social work has an impact on large and increasing number of citizens. A major aim of *Evaluative Studies in Social Work* is to increase well informed understanding of social work, based on knowledge about its real rather than imagined activities and outcomes.

The identification of effectiveness, in its various forms, can also not be the end of the story. The costs of the associated services must be studied, set in the context of their effectiveness, to allow the most efficient use of resources.

These demands present major challenges to researchers who have to use, adapt and develop a wide range of research methods and designs. Ingenuity and persistence are both required if evaluative research in social work is to be pursued in contexts often regarded as beyond the scope of such enquiry. *Evaluative Studies in Social Work* intends to make widely available not only the research findings about the impact of social work but also to demonstrate and discuss possible approaches and methods in this important and developing field of enquiry.

The volumes in this series so far describe studies undertaken in the Social Work Research Centre at the University of Stirling. Later volumes will include work carried out elsewhere. The Centre is funded by the Scottish Office to evaluate the effectiveness of social work services. It also receives substantial funds from other sources including the University and grants from the Economic and Social Research Council and charitable organisations.

Bail Services in Scotland is the third volume in the series which explores the impact of social work services within the criminal justice system. It focuses on matters which continue to challenge sentencers, policy makers and practitioners, not least because of the often vociferous public concern about crime, punishment and the administration of criminal justice. This concern, which is far more evident in some countries than others, may be exacerbated by political interests which see advantage in promises to crack down on actual or supposed increases in crime and on the alleged malpractices of prosecutors and sentencers.

Research which identifies what is really happening and the outcomes of the various interacting components of the criminal justice system does not, of course, guarantee that policies will actually be influenced by sound research; the evolution in the mid 1990's of some aspects of the English penal system demonstrates this well. However, in the aftermath of political squalls and the ensuing turmoil policy makers and practitioners have still to respond to the enduring problems. Evaluative research makes it possible for debate and difficult decisions to be properly informed. One purpose of this series is to make available detailed accounts of the often highly complex research needed to identify the immediate and longer term effects of public policy.

The administration of bail for people charged with or convicted of offences is an example of a complicated policy matter which raises important questions of justice and expediency. About a fifth of the UK prison population are on remand and they often experience some of the worst conditions within the prison system. Over a fifth of these people will eventually be acquitted and over a third, after they have been convicted, do not receive a custodial sentence. At the very least this would appear to add some unnecessary pressure on prisons which are seriously overcrowded, often unstable and extremely expensive. Inappropriate remands, especially those which are not followed by a prison sentence, can also be unjust in that people whom the courts deemed not to deserve a prison sentence actually received one.

This rather stark scenario must not obscure the difficult decisions prosecutors and sentencers face in reaching decisions about bail. There are legislative and other pressures on them to remand in custody sparingly but they have also to be reasonably confident that those bailed will attend their subsequent court appearances and that they will not interfere with witnesses or commit further offences while on bail. Some account must also be taken of public sensitivities about people who have allegedly committed serious crimes remaining in the community.

An individual's criminal history and the nature of the alleged offence are particularly influential striking this delicate balance but it is also known that domestic circumstances can play a part. Some of those with no ties or supervision may be thought to be at risk of failing to attend court; and those with no fixed abode are seen as particular risks. About 10 per cent of people remanded in custody have no accommodation when they first appear in court. The Scottish Office decided therefore to fund and to evaluate two experimental bail information and accommodation schemes. These would aim to target people thought especially likely to be remanded in custody and would provide information to courts designed to assist the more accurate identification of people who would be unlikely to abuse bail. Accommodation would also be offered to people with no fixed abode.

McIvor's and Warner's painstaking study of all aspects of these schemes and their various outcomes - from the esteem in which sentencers held them to the actual bail and custody decisions made and the subsequent breach of bail orders - show that the schemes succeeded in facilitating the granting of bail to accused people who would otherwise have been remanded in custody. This was achieved without increasing the risk of bail abuse. The schemes could not, however, make a significant impact on the total numbers of remands in custody because these decisions are influenced primarily by an individual's offending history and the actual offence. The study also demonstrated, however, how inexact these predictions are, and it points to ways in which the quality of bail decision making could be improved.

In its meticulous analysis of bail schemes in action and masterly review of what is now known about what can and cannot be achieved in preventing unnecessary custodial remands this volume is an excellent example of the contribution of evaluative research to policy making. And at a time when, in England at least, politicians want to narrow the scope and activities of the probation service *Bail Schemes in Scotland* also shows how social work can have a respected and useful place in the criminal justice system, bringing together impartial information for courts and help and supervision for offenders.

Juliet Cheetham
University of Stirling

xiv

Acknowledgements

We received a great deal of help and information from many sources in undertaking the research reported in this book. We cannot thank everyone by name, but special thanks are due to the staff in the bail schemes in Edinburgh and Glasgow, representatives of Lothian and Strathclyde Social Work Departments, members of the advisory groups, fiscals, sheriffs, sheriff clerks, police and defence agents. All were willing to talk to us at some length about the schemes and the associated issues.

We wish to thank in particular the bail officers, administrative staff, their line managers and colleagues. It is never easy setting up new projects and even harder with a research team following every move. Angela Feherty, Morag McCourtney, Stephen Madill and Chris Paxton, the bail officers, answered questions, explained procedure and dealt with an external evaluation with great humour and patience.

We also received a great deal of help from Sergeants Stewart Millar and William Nicol of the Scottish Criminal Record Office who provided information on criminal history, bail abuse and the final outcomes for bailees and custodial remands. We are similarly grateful to Fiona Paterson from the Central Research Unit at the Scottish Office for her help, advice and sympathetic ear throughout the research period.

Ann Netten and Martin Knapp wish also to thank the following for their help in researching the costs of the bail schemes: Neil Buchan, Graham Casey, Helen Clarke, Catherine Faulds, Sue Hancock, Fiona Hurd, Pete Lawrence, Jim Lillie, William Saddler and Isobel Stenhouse.

Thanks are finally due to Emmanuelle Tulle-Winton and Cheryl Burgess who undertook much of the data collection cheerfully and painstakingly and last, but of course not least, to our colleagues in the Social Work Research Centre, especially to Pam Lavery and June Watson who prepared the manuscript.

Acknowledgements

1 Introduction and background

Introduction

The question of which accused persons should be released on bail pending trial arises periodically. From the late 1950s onwards there have been a number of studies, working parties and changes to bail legislation and provision with a view to ensuring both that bail is both granted as often as possible and that those most at risk of breaching bail are remanded in custody. By the early 1980s concern was being expressed about the high levels of imprisonment in the United Kingdom, particularly with respect to remand prisoners. More recently, prison disturbances and, in England, the increasing use of police cells to detain remand prisoners have focused political and public attention on bail.

Three broad concerns relating to bail have been raised over the past forty years. These include protecting the rights of the accused person, protecting the public and facilitating the administration of justice. It is important for a variety of reasons that remands in custody only occur when there is no alternative: a custodial remand can severely disrupt the lives of prisoners and their families, yet a large proportion of those remanded in custody do not subsequently receive a custodial sentence. Unnecessary remands in custody also place a considerable burden on the prison system.

At the same time, however, high and rising levels of crime have been linked to offences committed by people on bail and the courts have been criticised for their lax attitude to the granting of bail. The costs to the public purse and the inconvenience to criminal justice staff, to the courts and to witnesses of accused persons failing to appear as required have also had an influence on the consideration of bail. These often conflicting concerns relate directly to the delicate balance that prosecutors and sentencers face when determining whether or not an accused person should be granted bail.

Various steps have been taken on both sides of the border to reduce the prison population in the United Kingdom. Schemes have been introduced to reduce the number of persons imprisoned for fine default. In Scotland, for example, this has included the development of the supervised attendance order as an alternative to imprisonment for default. Alternatives to direct custodial sentences (now community sentences in England and Wales) have developed apace since the introduction of community service orders in the 1970s. Such measures represent a conscious attempt to reduce the number of convicted offenders for whom a sentence of imprisonment is necessary. Finally, bail information schemes and other pre-trial services have been introduced with the specific aim of reducing the number of prisoners remanded in custody prior to sentence or trial.

This book examines in detail the operation of two Scottish bail information and accommodation schemes. Introduced in 1991, the schemes were aimed at providing the courts with social information concerning those at risk of being remanded in custody and, in appropriate cases, locating accommodation for accused persons so at risk. As such they attempted to impact positively upon the courts' willingness to grant bail to accused persons who might otherwise be remanded in custody.

The present chapter describes the context within which pre-trial services in the United Kingdom have been developed and operate. A more detailed discussion of the bail process can be found in Cavadino and Gibson (1993) and, with respect to Scotland, in Paterson and Whittaker (1994) and Paterson (1996a).

Bail and custodial remand in England and Wales

Once a person has been charged with an offence in England and Wales, the defendant can be held in custody to appear at court on the next working day or be granted bail to appear at court on a given date. Since the implementation of the Criminal Justice and Public Order Act 1994 in 1995, the police have also had the power to attach specific conditions to police bail. Burrows et al. (1994) found that around 60 per cent of persons charged were given police bail, while 40 per cent were held in police custody.

When a defendant appears in court the court must decide, if the case is adjourned, whether to grant unconditional bail or bail with one or more conditions or whether to remand the person in custody until the next hearing. Prior to such a decision being reached the Crown Prosecution Service may make recommendations to the court as to whether bail should be refused or specific conditions attached to a bail order. In 1992 around one in nine defendants were remanded in custody during Magistrate court proceedings. By comparison, 22 per cent of defendants committed for trial to the Crown Court were committed for trial in custody (Home Office, 1993).

The 1976 Bail Act has as its basis a presumption in favour of bail unless there are grounds for believing that if bailed the defendant would fail to appear at court when required, would commit an offence while on bail or would interfere with witnesses or otherwise obstruct the course of justice. However, the court's decision is strongly influenced by the earlier police decision (Burrows et al., 1994; Jones, 1985). If the police grant bail after charging a suspect, the Crown Prosecution Service rarely opposes unconditional bail in court and the court rarely questions or refuses the granting of unconditional bail.

As early as the late 1950s research conducted in England and Wales highlighted problems with decision-making in relation to the bail process. The decision regarding bail was said to be hurried and often based on minimal information, the result being that too many accused persons were needlessly remanded in custody to the detriment of their personal life and to the final outcome of the case. Gibson (cited in Melvin and Didcott, 1976) found that a high proportion of those remanded in custody in England did not subsequently receive a custodial sentence and that the remand population at that time was placing an increasing burden on the prison system.

In 1992 remand prisoners awaiting trial or sentence in penal establishments or police cells in England and Wales constituted 22 per cent of the average prison population, with around a fifth of remands awaiting sentence and four-fifths awaiting trial (Cavadino and Gibson, 1993). Hedderman (1991) showed that being remanded in custody was an important predictor of later custodial sentences, even when controlling for other variables which have a bearing upon sentencing outcomes. This said, however, prison statistics for 1991 indicated that 36 per cent of all defendants - 35 per cent of male defendants and 53 per cent of females - remanded in custody for whom the outcome was recorded did not subsequently receive a custodial sentence (Home Office, 1993). Cavadino and Gibson (1993) have suggested that this figure is likely to be an underestimate because those for whom the outcome was not recorded were unlikely to have been sentenced to custody. Instead, they would have been acquitted or have received a non-custodial sentence. Home Office figures for 1992, however, revealed that 21 per cent of persons remanded in custody were acquitted and 39 per cent received a non-custodial disposal (Home Office, 1993). Although it has been argued that the proportion in the first group should, in the interests of justice, be kept as low as possible, it is also recognised that some of the latter group may have been given custodial sentences if they had not already spent some time in custody on remand (Morgan, 1996).

Cavadino and Gibson (1993, p.76) have succinctly summarised the situation of remand prisoners in England and Wales as follows:

> At the end of their time on remand a high proportion of untried
> prisoners are found not guilty or given non-custodial sentences. In other
> words, they are judged not to deserve a prison sentence; yet they have
> effectively already served one, and have done so in some of the most
> squalid parts of our penal system. Moreover, their experience of pre-trial
> imprisonment may- through loss of employment, accommodation, family
> and other community ties - have increased the likelihood of subsequent
> offending.

To illustrate this point more starkly the authors point to the fact that while
remand prisoners constitutes just over a fifth of the average prison population
between 1988-92, they comprised 47 per cent of the prisoners who committed
suicide during that period.

However, just as the quality of information available to bail decision-
makers might result in the remanding in custody of defendants for whom such
a course of action is unnecessary, either to facilitate the administration of
justice or to protect the public, so must decision-makers have regard to the
possibility of bail abuse if a defendant is released. Decision-makers have to
assess the likelihood that if released on bail, a defendant will breach the
conditions of that release either by failing to appear at court, by otherwise
interfering with the administration of justice or by committing further offences
whilst on bail.

In the early 1990s the issue of bail abuse, particularly with respect to
offending on bail, became a matter of considerable debate. A number of
studies into offending on bail were published by police forces and were
utilised by the police to argue for changes to be made to the bail legislation.
Chief Constables in England and Wales called for tighter bail regulations to
counteract car crimes and burglaries committed by young offenders on bail and
for the creation of a new offence of breach of bail. They argued that more
information should be made available to the courts to encourage the use of
remands in custody for prolific offenders (Carvel, 1991). Such concerns were
not, however, confined to south of the border. In Scotland it was claimed at
the Police Federation Annual Conference in 1991 that the existing bail
legislation had lost its impact and respect (The Herald, 1991). The Chief
Constable for Lothian and Borders Police expressed criticism of courts which
released on bail accused persons who subsequently re-offended (Lothian and
Borders Police, 1992) and a Labour Member of Parliament blamed 'bail-happy
sheriffs' for the current crime-wave (The Daily Record, 1992).

The response from the Home Office in England was to state that tougher measures would be taken with respect to 'bail bandits' while at the same time avoiding placing increasing pressure on the prison system. In February 1992 the Home Secretary indicated that a number of new measures would be introduced. Legislation would be introduced to make bail offences an aggravating factor at sentence; the police would be given statutory powers to arrest immediately anyone allegedly in breach of bail; accused persons would be warned in court that breach of bail could result in a custodial remand; new bail information projects would be developed to ensure that those likely to offend were not granted bail; training in risk assessment would be provided to magistrates; and, finally, eight million pounds would be made available for bail accommodation and support (Carvel, 1992; NACRO, 1992). A number of these proposals were introduced in the Criminal Justice and Public Order Act 1994.

Studies of the actual levels of bail abuse suggest a somewhat different picture, though comparing the level of bail abuse across different geographical areas and at different points in time is complicated by a number of factors (Morgan, 1992). Changes in police practice with respect to the recording of bail abuse, for example, may account to an unknown extent for apparent changes in its incidence over time. Cross-study comparisons are likewise limited by the use of different measures of bail abuse. For these reasons, studies of bail abuse have been subject to criticism by the National Association of Probation Officers (NAPO, 1991) and NACRO (1992).

A study conducted by Northumbria Police in 1989 showed that 17 per cent of bailees in the area were cautioned for or found guilty of new offences or had such offences taken into consideration (Northumbria Police, 1991). These figures, however, related to arrests, not all of which led to a charge or conviction and, as such, they do not provide an accurate indication of actual levels of offending on bail. The Northumbria study also revealed that 31 per cent of crimes in North Tyneside which were 'cleared up' by police were found to be committed by persons on bail. In Greater Manchester (Greater Manchester Police, 1988) and in Avon and Somerset (Brookes, 1991), 23 per cent and 29 per cent respectively of those charged with offences were on bail when charged or arrested. Finally, a study conducted by the Metropolitan Police found that only 12 per cent of people on bail were convicted of further offences and it was estimated that 16 per cent of all detected offences were committed by persons on bail (Ennis and Nichols, 1991).

A review of recent studies of bail abuse in England and Wales concluded that whilst the numbers bailed and the numbers of accused who had offended on bail had both increased, the proportion of accused who had offended on bail had remained constant at around 10 per cent outwith London and 12 per cent in London. Re-offending on bail was found to be highest among individuals charged with offences involving theft of or from a motor vehicle and burglary

(23 per cent and 20 per cent respectively). It was lowest among those charged with offences involving violence (between six and eight per cent). When the police were opposed to bail and the accused was subsequently granted bail, 18 per cent of persons re-offended on bail. This compared with a nine per cent re-offending rate for those for whom the police did not oppose bail. However, most of those identified as being at high risk of offending on bail (17 to 20 year olds who had committed theft of or from cars or burglary) were not charged with the commission of further offences whilst on bail.

The finding that most people do not breach the conditions of a bail order is compatible with earlier research. For example, a Home Office study showed that nine per cent of those bailed from Magistrates Courts in England and Wales were subsequently convicted of an offence committed whilst on bail (Home Office, 1981).

Melvin and Didcott (1976) likewise found in their study of bail and custodial remands in Scotland that most accused did not breach bail. Eight per cent of the sample abused their release on bail either by absconding or by committing further offences. More recently, Wozniak et al. (1988) reported a sharp increase in Scotland in the number of bail offences (most of which related to offending on bail) during the first half of the 1980s. However, most of this increase was likely to be accounted for by changes in police practice with respect to the recording of offences committed on bail. The Bail (Etc) Scotland Act 1980 introduced a new substantive offence of bail abuse with which bailees could be charged in addition to any new offences allegedly committed on bail.

Most people do not, therefore, abuse bail. Moreover, the level of bail abuse has, it appears, remained broadly constant despite increasing numbers of persons released on bail, changes in bail legislation and in the ways in which the police record abuse of bail. This said, it has to be acknowledged that since only a minority of crimes are cleared up by the police, the level of recorded bail abuse will serve to underestimate the number of actual offences committed by bailees.

The numbers of defendants remanded in custody in England and Wales increased by 43 per cent between 1979 and 1987 while the average length of stay rose by 60 per cent during the same period (Morgan, 1996). Whilst there is no disputing the pressure that the scale of the resulting remand population placed upon prisons and upon the police, Morgan has argued that there is little evidence that the increased remand population during the 1980s was caused by increased severity on the part of the courts. The decrease in the remand population between 1989 and 1992, on the other hand, she attributes partly to the growth in bail information schemes and in the number of bail hostel places available to the courts.

The history and development of bail information schemes

Bail information schemes aim to provide independent factual, verified information relating to accused persons held in police custody prior to a court appearance the following day. The first independent bail service was based in Manhattan and was established by the Vera Foundation (now the Vera Institute for Justice) in New York in 1960. The Manhattan Bail Project was developed to reduce the use of custodial remand related to an accused person's inability to pay bonds to secure release. The aim was to decrease the use of bail bonds and increase the number of individuals released on unconditional bail. This was to be achieved by providing the courts with verified information relating to the accused person's social and community ties, including their family situation, employment status and health.

Trainee lawyers interviewed accused held in police custody prior to their court appearance. Information was collected on the accused person's community ties and points were allocated for different pieces of information. If the case scored sufficient points, scheme staff recommended that the accused be granted bail. They also took steps to remind accused of forthcoming court appearances in an attempt to impact positively upon the incidence of failure to appear. The scheme was found to be successful in decreasing the use of bail bonds and increasing the use of bail without increasing the non-appearance rate at court (Rankin and Sturz, 1971).

In 1975 the Vera Institute, in co-operation with the Home Office and the Inner London Probation Service, set up an experimental bail information scheme in Camberwell. During the 1970s a total of 16 similar schemes were developed (Williams, 1992). However, interest in bail information gradually declined. Williams (1992) has suggested that this was at least partly due to a lack of extra funding being made available for bail information services. Opposition to further expansion of bail services was also voiced by probation officers and magistrates.

Godson and Mitchell (1991) have suggested that there were several reasons why, despite the success of the Camberwell scheme, no further schemes were developed for several years: the tasks involved became purely administrative and community resources for bailees were not developed; probation officers became more community-based and spent less time in the courts; there was an assumption that legislation embodied in the 1976 Bail Act would solve problems related to the remand population; the Duty Solicitor Scheme was introduced; there was a lack of clarity as to whom bail information should be given; and there was, at the time, no crisis related to custodial remand or the size of the prison population.

By the mid 1980s, however, bail and custodial remand was again an issue in the United Kingdom, particularly in England and Wales. Prompted by a rising prison population, prison disturbances and, in England and Wales, the costs and pressures of keeping prisoners in police cells, policy makers again focused attention on the use of bail.

In 1986 the Association of Chief Officers of Probation (ACOP) and the Vera Institute for Justice produced a joint paper on the development of bail information schemes. The timing of the report was closely related to the introduction of the Crown Prosecution Service (CPS) in England and Wales, which took over the role of public prosecutor from the police. One of the roles of the CPS was to review information pertinent to the bail decision and to make recommendations regarding bail to the courts. There was now, therefore, a body with a clear role with respect to bail decision-making who might usefully draw upon bail information in this process.

The ACOP/Vera paper recommended that bail information schemes, run by probation services, be introduced on an experimental basis and by early 1987 eight pilot schemes had been introduced. The general approach adopted by schemes was that bail information officers interviewed defendants who had been detained in police custody and whose bail would be opposed by the police. The interviews were aimed at eliciting information about community ties which was then verified by the bail officer and a report submitted to the CPS and to the defence.

The schemes were monitored by Vera staff and were said to have been effective in increasing the use of bail by the courts (Stone, 1988). Stone's research indicated that out of 1367 cases in which bail information was provided, 874 defendants were granted bail. He estimated that 400 of these defendants had been bailed as a direct consequence of bail information provided by the schemes. In other words, between a quarter and a third of bail information reports had been influential in ensuring that the defendant was diverted from a custodial remand.

In less than two years bail information schemes were operational in 45 magistrates courts and in five prisons (ACOP, 1990). By 1994 there were 193 court-based schemes and 38 prison-based schemes in existence (Mair and Lloyd, 1996). Mair and Lloyd have observed that, in contrast with other probation initiatives, the national development of bail information schemes - which was based on an agreement between ACOP, the Crown Prosecution Service, the police and the Home Office - was characterised by a high degree of careful planning and co-operation. The extension of bail information schemes was managed by a National Steering Group, chaired by the Home Office and concerned with overall strategic issues and by the ACOP Practice Committee with responsibility for more detailed operational issues and the official approval of schemes.

Godson and Mitchell (1991), in their analysis of monitoring data provided by schemes, found that the Crown Prosecution Service was more likely to reject police requests for a remand in custody if verified information was available. When such information was available, defence agents were also more likely to request bail and to do so successfully. However, a problem was identified in relation to the targeting of reports: a number of reports were submitted in cases in which the police did not request a custodial remand. On the basis of their review, Godson and Mitchell were reluctant to draw firm conclusions about the effectiveness of the English bail schemes in reducing the use of custodial remands, arguing that to do so would 'obscure their primary purpose which is to provide information to the CPS' (p. 34).

In 1992 the Home Office Research and Planning Unit published a detailed study of four bail information schemes (Lloyd, 1992). The main aims of the study were to evaluate the extent to which the bail schemes had succeeded in diverting unnecessary remands and to assess how their effectiveness related to the organisation of the schemes. Three of the schemes were located in Magistrates Courts and the fourth was prison-based. The work of the schemes was monitored for a six-month period, interviews were conducted with bail officers and with other staff from relevant agencies and the work of the schemes was observed.

The study revealed that the bail information schemes had been successful in influencing bail decisions and had served to divert a proportion of defendants from a custodial remand. The court-based schemes were, however, found to be effective in different ways by having their influence at different points in the bail decision-making process. One scheme had its influence primarily through providing the defence with a stronger case in favour of bail, the second had most effect by removing Crown opposition to bail, while the third scheme was influential at both of these points in the bail process. Lloyd found that the scheme which had an influence both on the CPS and on the strength of defence applications for bail was most effective in increasing the use made of bail by the courts. The prison scheme, which focused on defendants who were remanded in custody at first appearance, was found to be effective in diverting accused from subsequent custodial remands.

Consistent with these findings, a Probation Inspectorate report published in 1993 concluded that 'bail information schemes had been a significant influence on the Crown Prosecution Service's recommendation on the use of bail and are cost effective' (HM Inspectorate of Probation, 1993, para. 3.7). Concern has been expressed, however, that bail information schemes might lead to an increase in bail abuse if they are successful in securing the release of more remand prisoners. This issue was addressed in the studies by Lloyd (1992) and

9

by Stone (1988). Stone found that in most schemes, those released on bail and for whom bail information had been provided were not more likely subsequently to abuse bail. There were, however, two schemes in which bailees who had bail information provided were more likely to be arrested in comparison with those for whom no bail information had been available. Lloyd examined bail abuse by recording those cases which appeared more than once through the bail schemes on the grounds that defendants arrested for offences committed whilst on bail were likely to be remanded in custody. He found that 11 per cent of those for whom bail information was made available to bail decision-makers subsequently re-appeared in the scheme for having allegedly committed an offence on bail. This compared with ten per cent of those for whom verified information about community ties was not available. Excluding accused who were subsequently granted bail (on the grounds that the offence allegedly committed on bail was trivial since the accused would otherwise have been remanded in custody) seven per cent of both groups were alleged to have breached bail. When all types of bail abuse were taken into account, six per cent of the bail information group were alleged to have breached bail compared with eight per cent of those for whom such information was not available to bail decision-makers.

Bail accommodation

Research in Britain has consistently suggested that those involved in the prosecution of alleged offences are primarily concerned with assessing the likelihood that the accused will commit further offences if liberated pending trial, with the likelihood of absconding being accorded secondary importance (Melvin and Didcott, 1976; Paterson and Whittaker, 1994). In bail decision-making, particular weight is therefore ascribed to factors related to the accused person's criminal history and to the current offence. This suggests that bail information might have a limited contribution to make to the bail decision-making process. Several studies have, however, demonstrated that the availability or otherwise of a fixed address can be an important determinant of attitudes towards the granting of bail.

In Melvin and Didcott's (1976) study, for instance, prosecutors were opposed to the granting of bail in around ten per cent of cases on the grounds that the accused was of no fixed abode. Wozniak et al. (1988), in a study which focused on the remand population in Scottish prisons on one day in 1984, reported that bail had been opposed by the fiscal in 14 per cent of cases on the grounds that the accused was of no fixed abode. The finding that a lower proportion of these cases subsequently received a custodial sentence in comparison with other accused for whom the availability of an address had not been an issue caused the authors to question the appropriateness of remanding accused persons in custody on the basis of their lack of a fixed address.

In his study of four English bail information schemes, Lloyd (1992) reported that between 15 and 30 per cent of those interviewed by the schemes were recorded as being of no fixed abode (hostel dwellers were counted as a separate category). In their study of another four schemes, Godson and Mitchell (1991) found an average no fixed abode (NFA) rate of 12 per cent, with differences between the schemes ranging from five to 22 per cent.

Given the relevance of address to the bail decision it is perhaps surprising that bail information schemes do not appear to have actively targeted cases in which the defendant is of no fixed abode. This is particularly so in view of the finding that bail information can be used effectively in such cases (e.g. Lloyd, 1992; Morgan, 1992). In Lloyd's study 72 per cent of those who were of no fixed abode and for whom bail information was available were granted bail compared with 15 per cent of defendants of no fixed abode for whom such information was not available. Bail information also appeared to be useful in cases in which the defendant was resident outwith the locality. Bail information was more effective, however, in securing defendants identified by the bail information schemes as being of no fixed abode and less so in cases in which bail information was opposed by the police on the basis of the defendant's address.

Definitions may vary, however, as to what counts as a fixed address. In their study of bail hostels in London, for instance, Lewis and Mair (1988) suggested that the police may have defined as being of no fixed abode defendants who were living in squats or in temporary rented accommodation which for other purposes would be considered to constitute a secure address.

The issue of where an accused person lives is of relevance to the bail decision for two reasons: to ensure that documents can be served and to ensure the accused appears at court. Bail accommodation aims to address the needs of defendants who have nowhere to live or who are otherwise unable to offer an acceptable address and by so doing to reduce the incidence of unnecessary custodial remands.

Since the introduction of the 1972 Criminal Justice Act, courts in England and Wales have been able to attach to a bail order the condition that an accused person reside in a hostel. Limited information is available with respect to the use of bail accommodation, Lloyd's (1992) research into bail schemes being one exception. Lloyd found that the schemes varied in terms of the success of bail accommodation, though all relied mainly on hostels in which to place bailees rather than using facilities such as bed and breakfast accommodation.

11

In two schemes, based in Blackpool and Manchester, accommodation placements were made through a central point. In Blackpool there were no local hostels and referrals would not be accepted unless the magistrate was known to be considering bail. In such instances the case was stood down to await acceptance at a hostel, with the result that cases could be considerably delayed. Bail staff had previously made use of their own network of accommodation providers and had been able to place accused persons in appropriate provision.

In Manchester by contrast, referrals were accepted by the central placement unit on the basis of limited information. There were five bail hostels available in the area and use could also be made of voluntary sector provision. The only difficulty arose in relation to finding accommodation for 17 and 18 year olds with no previous convictions; bail hostels encouraged referrals from serious offenders and, since these young people often had no entitlement to state benefit, use could not be made of guest houses.

The third court-based scheme, based in Hull, dealt with relatively few accused of no fixed abode but had access to probation service and voluntary sector hostels. The success of schemes in accessing bail accommodation appeared, therefore, to be related both to what was locally available and to the existence of an efficient referral mechanism which enabled bail staff to inform the courts as quickly as possible that accommodation was available.

Some hostels provide accommodation for people on probation orders but make available bed spaces for defendants on bail. Accommodation in probation hostels is often made available to bailees following conviction and prior to sentence to assess the person's suitability for residence in the hostel or to facilitate the preparation of reports.

Lewis and Mair (1988), in their study of hostels in London, reported that they differed in their treatment of bailees and in the amount of help or support offered to residents. Some simply provided defendants on bail with accommodation, while others were more controlling of bailees and their activities. Their study also highlighted difficulties faced by hostels in accommodating bailees. These included the tension between maintaining high occupancy rates while making available to the courts at short notice accommodation which might not subsequently be taken up; the availability of limited information about defendants at the point of referral; and the impact on the manageability of the hostel when accepting new residents at short notice. Finally, Lewis and Mair found a discrepancy between hostel policy and practice and questioned whether, had they not been offered a placement, many residents would otherwise have been remanded in custody.

The development of bail services in Scotland

Following the apprehension and arrest of a suspect, police in Scotland have several options if the case is to be pursued. The accused can be detained in police custody until appearing in court on the next lawful day, released on a written undertaking to appear at a specified court at a specified time, or liberated pending a summons from the procurator fiscal (the public prosecutor). Guidance issued to the police based on the Lord Advocate's guidelines (the Wheatley guidelines) indicates that accused should be detained if their identity is in doubt; if they are required for further enquiries; if they are of no fixed abode; if they are thought likely to commit offences if released; or of they are unable (through, for example, the influence of alcohol or drugs) to understand or agree to the terms of an undertaking.

Generally the accused will be liberated if the offence is trivial, of he or she has a fixed address and is thought unlikely to re-offend. As well as considering factors outlined in the Bail (Etc) Scotland Act 1980 and elaborated by the Wheatley guidelines (see p.15), the police take into consideration the accused person's criminal record, including conduct during previous bail orders, and the nature and context of the offence. Serious cases likely to be dealt with by solemn procedures are generally detained. Juveniles are treated differently: they are held in separate accommodation and seen by the Superintendent. The police are reluctant to detain juveniles, but are unable to release them unless it is into the custody of a responsible adult.

If the accused person does not have a fixed address, then she or he will be detained in custody until one can be located or verified. In most cases involving less serious offences the court simply needs to be satisfied that the accused can provide an address to which documents can be sent - a domicile of citation - to facilitate the administration of justice. If the accused is alleged to have committed an offence at or near to her or his home address, detention can, in the short term at least, prevent further offending which might otherwise have occurred if the accused had returned home.

When detained in police custody accused persons will be asked if they wish a solicitor to be informed. In most cases the defence agent will visit the accused immediately before the case is heard in court. Legal aid is available at first appearance in all courts through a duty solicitor scheme.

On the morning of the next lawful day, accused persons are transported to the cells in the sheriff court to await their appearance. If a further hearing is necessary (that is, unless a guilty plea is tendered and the accused sentenced) the court has three options available to it at this stage: to ordain the accused to appear at court at a future date; to bail the accused; or to remand the accused in custody. Those who are subject to a further remand in custody are transferred to local prisons after their court appearance.

An accused may be released by the court subject to the standard conditions of bail: to appear at court at the appointed time; to refrain from committing offences; not to interfere with witnesses or otherwise obstruct the course of justice; and to make themselves available for further enquiries or the preparation of reports for the court. The court may, in addition, attach specific conditions to a bail order if this is thought necessary to protect the public or to facilitate the administration of justice.

All prosecutions in Scotland are undertaken on behalf of the Crown by the procurator fiscal. The fiscal decides on the basis of police reports whether or not a case should be prosecuted and, if so, in which court and on what charges. The fiscal is also responsible for indicating whether or not the Crown is opposed to the accused being granted bail.

When an accused is appearing in court from police custody the fiscal's attitude to bail is recorded on case papers along with the reasons for any opposition to bail and whether or not the Crown will appeal the bail decision if the sheriff grants bail despite fiscal opposition. Fiscal opposition is central in determining whether or not the accused is granted bail

Although bail can only be granted by the court in Scotland, the decisions of police and fiscals will crucially affect the court's response to bail (Paterson, 1996b). Unless bail is opposed by the fiscal, then it will almost certainly be granted by the court. Where bail is opposed by the Crown and requested by the accused the sheriff considers the arguments for and against bail. This involves balancing the largely legal factors against bail put forward by the fiscal with defence arguments concerning the consequences of refusing bail.

In the less serious cases dealt with through summary procedures, an accused person who has been refused bail will be held in custody until the trial unless a successful appeal is subsequently lodged through the defence agent. Where bail is granted by the sheriff despite fiscal opposition, the Crown can appeal against the decision. Under these circumstances the accused will be remanded in custody pending the outcome of the appeal and cannot apply for bail in the interim. Bail appeals are heard by the High Court.

More serious cases are dealt with through solemn procedures. At first appearance accused generally make no plea or declaration and, if bail is not granted, will be remanded in custody for a week to enable further enquiries to be pursued. When the accused is remanded for further enquiries this decision cannot be appealed.

At this stage the court has two main concerns: ensuring that the accused will attend court as required (ensuring the administration of justice) and ensuring that the accused, if released into the community, will not commit offences (protecting the public). These basic aims underpin the Bail (Etc)

Scotland Act 1980 which, though primarily concerned with the abolition of money bail (the system under which an accused person lodges money to secure bail), was also expected to lead to a reduction in the number of prisoners held on remand (SACRO, 1987). In a study of bail and custodial remand in Scotland, Melvin and Didcott (1976) had advocated the introduction of a more liberal bail policy on the grounds that most accused who were judged to be 'bad risks' did not, in fact, abuse their release on bail. The 1980 Act also created a new offence covering the breach of bail conditions wherein police have the power of arrest if they have reasonable grounds for suspecting that the accused has broken, is breaking or is likely to break any condition imposed on his or her bail.

Scottish case law has established a presumption in favour of bail except in cases of treason or murder. Other exceptions were, however, set out in the Wheatley guidelines (Smith v McCallum, 1982). Taking as a starting point the assumption that an accused should be granted a bail order unless it can be shown that there are good grounds for not granting it, the Wheatley guidelines indicated that bail should be refused if such a course of action was deemed necessary to protect the public and ensure the administration of justice. The guidelines also indicated that bail should be refused if the accused was 'in a position of trust to behave as a good citizen and not to breach the law'. There should, therefore, be a presumption against bail being granted if the accused was already on bail or ordained to appear in respect of other offences or was subject to probation, a community service order or a deferred sentence. The Criminal Justice (Scotland) Act 1995 subsequently removed the presumption of bail for people convicted of culpable homicide, attempted murder, rape and attempted rape where they have a previous conviction for any of these offences or a previous conviction for murder.

In late 1980 a study was undertaken to examine the immediate impact of the 1980 Bail Act (Moody, 1980). Thirty one per cent of all those arrested during a three week period were found to have been detained in police custody, mostly related to alleged offences of violence or housebreaking. There was, however, considerable variation between police divisions in the use made of detention, ranging from 12 per cent to 63 per cent of arrests. The most common reason for police detention was the absence of a fixed address, followed by the seriousness of the alleged offence, the fact that the accused was already on bail and an assessment that the accused was likely to commit further offences if released.

Moody found that the fiscal agreed to bail being granted in 53 per cent of cases in which it was requested (bail was not requested at first appearance in just over half the cases). If the fiscal had a favourable attitude to bail it was rarely refused by the court. However bail was refused by the court in 60 per cent of cases in which the granting of bail was opposed by the fiscal. Very few accused (three per cent) were remanded after their initial appearance, largely as a consequence of the high rate of guilty pleas taken at first appearance.

The reasons provided for fiscal opposition to bail related primarily to the accused person's criminal record or to factors associated with the current offence (see also Paterson and Whittaker, 1994; Paterson, 1996b). There was a high degree of consistency between the reasons for police detention and for fiscal opposition to bail.

In a study conducted by the Scottish Office, relevant data were collected for two months before the introduction of the 1980 Act and for a one-year period afterwards (SHHD, 1981). The study showed that, following the introduction of the 1980 Act, the numbers held in police detention fell by ten per cent as police made more use of their powers to release accused persons on citation or on a written undertaking to appear at court. Again, however, there was found to be considerable variation in the use made of detention by the police.

The research conducted by Wozniak et al. (1988) focused on all persons remanded in custody on 11th December 1984. On that date, remand prisoners constituted 22 per cent of the total population and 71 per cent of those on remand were awaiting trial. Sixty-one per cent of the sample subsequently received a custodial sentence, while in 11 per cent of cases the accused was found not guilty, a not proven verdict was returned or the case was not proceeded with. The remaining accused received non-custodial sentences. Women and younger people who had been remanded in custody were less likely than other accused subsequently to be imprisoned. An apparent relationship was found between the length of time on remand and the final outcome of the case: the longer the period in custody, the greater the likelihood of a custodial sentence being passed.

The study also examined the factors relevant to the fiscals' attitude to bail, in a random sub-sample of cases. In 57 per cent of cases the fiscal opposed bail primarily or solely on the basis of the accused person's criminal history and/or because of the serious nature of the offence. In 52 per cent of cases breach of trust was a factor in the decision to oppose bail (that is, the accused was currently on bail, subject to a probation or community service order or on a deferred sentence at the time of the alleged offence). Bail was opposed on the basis of lack of a fixed address in 14 per cent of cases. An accused person was more likely to receive a custodial sentence if breach of trust or criminal history were factors in the fiscal's decision to oppose bail. Where bail had been opposed on the basis of the accused person's lack of a fixed address or because of the need for further enquiries a custodial sentence was less likely.

Despite the hope that the 1980 Act would result in a reduction in the numbers of remand prisoners, the remand population in Scotland continued to increase between 1980 and 1985, with most of the increase relating to the pre-trial population. By the mid 1980s Scotland had the second highest remand population in Europe. Wozniak et al. (1988) suggested that the growth in the remand population was, in the years up until 1984, largely a reflection of an increase in average time spent on custodial remand. The later increase between 1984 and 1985, however, appeared to be related to an increase in the numbers remanded in custody by the courts. They concluded that the increase in the remand population over that period was not a result of rising crime rates or busier courts. Even though the remand population decreased between 1985 and 1990 the number of remand receptions increased slightly in 1990. In that year remand prisoners still accounted for 16 per cent of all prisoners in Scottish prisons and 47 per cent of all receptions to penal establishments (Scottish Office, 1992a).

In 1987 a working group appointed by the Scottish Association for the Care and Resettlement of Offenders (SACRO) published a report on bail and custodial remand. The working group was established to 'examine the factors relating to bail and custodial remand, both pre-trial and after conviction, and to review the conditions within remand institutions and to make recommendations' (SACRO, 1987, p.1). It concluded that the 1980 Act had not led to a substantial reduction in custodial remands, either prior to trial or awaiting sentence, and that the high level of remands in custody (44 per cent of all receptions in 1985) had an adverse effect on conditions in Scottish prisons, with both the daily number of custodial remands and the number of annual receptions rising steadily between 1979 and 1985. Visits to remand establishments revealed that the conditions in which remand prisoners were held were poor. Remand prisoners were acknowledged by prison governors as often experiencing worse conditions than convicted prisoners, including having few opportunities for recreation or work.

The working group suggested that the Wheatley guidelines had had the effect of restricting the use of bail and that they had been invoked to disallow the granting of bail even when an alleged offence committed by an accused on bail was trivial. It was also argued that the guidelines placed more pressure upon accused persons to plead guilty in order to avoid a further remand in custody.

The working group expressed concern that Scottish Office figures published in 1976 indicated that 70 per cent of accused persons recorded as being of no fixed abode were refused bail and suggested that the introduction of bail accommodation, including bail hostels, might have a positive impact on the level of custodial remand.

Melvin and Didcott's (1976) research had revealed that the use of custodial remands was related to the existence of weak community ties on the part of the accused. A remand in custody was more likely if the accused was of no fixed abode, was unemployed or had an 'unconventional' home life. Such factors were, however, secondary to criminal factors, such as previous convictions, when the fiscal formed an attitude towards the granting of bail. This led Melvin and Didcott (p.26) to conclude that:

...there would appear to be only limited scope for the simple introduction in Scotland of a Vera type of scoring system which is ... concerned principally with the strength of 'community ties' and consequent absconding risk.

The SACRO working group nevertheless recommended the appointment in the principal courts of bail supervision officers with a responsibility for the 'provision of information in relation to the granting of bail' and 'the supervision of those granted bail and identified by the court as requiring more active and continued oversight' (SACRO, 1987, p.24). In addition, the working group recommended that 'local authorities (possibly in conjunction with voluntary organisations) should undertake experimental projects for the provision of bail hostel and bail bed provision. Agreement should be sought with the Scottish Office regarding appropriate funding' (SACRO, 1987, p.25).

In the 1988 Kenneth Younger Memorial Lecture to the Howard League (Scotland) Malcolm Rifkind, the then Secretary of State, outlined the problems facing the Scottish penal system and the policies which were being developed to address them. In particular, he focused upon the need to reduce the unnecessary use of imprisonment on conviction, for fine default and prior to sentencing or trial. This concern was prompted by a recent history of unrest in Scottish penal establishments and by a recognition of the disruptive impact of imprisonment on offenders' lives. Pointing to the large number of short custodial remands, the then Scottish Secretary (Rifkind, 1989, p.87) indicated that:

...from pilot work and from the work by SACRO on options for bail accommodation we have concluded that an experiment in the provision of a bail information service combined with bail accommodation is worth serious consideration and might demonstrate whether such facilities should be worth promoting throughout Scotland.

In late 1989 the Scottish Office invited tenders for the development of pilot bail information and accommodation schemes. In early 1990 Lothian and Strathclyde Social Work Departments submitted successful proposals for such schemes, based on brief feasibility studies and following consultation with various agencies connected with the bail process. Both proposals involved a partnership between the social work department and SACRO.

The two pilot schemes focused upon the main sheriff courts in each region and became operational during 1991. Because of the experimental status of the initiative, it was subjected to an independent evaluation which forms the basis of the present volume.

Methodology

Description of scheme objectives and procedures

The overall aim of this aspect of the research was to gain an understanding of the way in which the schemes operated, their operational objectives and the services provided. First, written material relating to the schemes, including policy documents and minutes of meetings, was examined to chart the development of the schemes and to identify issues and problems which arose.

Interviews were conducted with staff, management and advisory group members. These were based on semi-structured interview schedules and interviewees were encouraged to discuss their perspectives, expectations and experiences of the bail schemes.

The practice of the bail staff was observed on several occasions. This was done in an informal, unstructured manner to provide a general picture of the approach taken in bail interviews and verification and to gain a clearer understanding of the day-to-day operation of the schemes.

The researchers attended advisory group meetings in order to observe informally the ways in which the members of different agencies responded to issues and problems and to gain more insight into the details of discussions in the groups.

Informal interviews were conducted with bail officers at various points during the evaluation in order to chart the progress of the schemes and to examine how difficulties which emerged were conceptualised and dealt with.

Finally, advisory group members were interviewed twice, shortly after the schemes became operational and again after they had been established for some time (after one year in Edinburgh and around six months in Glasgow). Interviews were conducted using semi-structured interview schedules and were aimed at eliciting members' expectations and experiences of the bail schemes.

Monitoring

All new cases dealt with by the schemes were monitored for a nine month period in Edinburgh and for five months in Glasgow. The shorter monitoring period in Glasgow resulted from the later introduction of that scheme. Data were collected from worksheets used by the bail officers. These were adapted from forms which had been widely used in the national monitoring of bail schemes in England and Wales. The nature of the monitoring exercise was discussed with bail staff to ensure that information collection did not interfere with the development of the services and to avoid duplication of data collection.

The types of information collected from worksheets included: details of the characteristics of accused persons dealt with by the schemes (for example age, sex and alleged offences); the types of information verified and the sources of verification; the reasons for non-submission of reports; the point at which bail services were provided, details of the fiscal's attitude to bail, remand decisions and, where possible, final outcome; details of referrals for accommodation.

The impact on the criminal justice system

The impact of the bail experiment was assessed in various ways. Semi-structured interviews were conducted with key agents in the criminal justice process. Representatives on the advisory groups were, as has already been indicated, interviewed on two occasions. Semi-structured interviews were also conducted with samples of sheriffs (four each in Edinburgh and Glasgow), depute fiscals with experience of marking custody cases (four each in Edinburgh and Glasgow), and defence agents who had had contact with the bail schemes (again four each in Edinburgh and Glasgow). These interviews were aimed at assessing the views of different groups as to the operation and effectiveness of the schemes and to the impact (if any) of the bail schemes on their own work.

The evaluation included a two-week period of observation in each court. Court observation was conducted in late 1991 and was included in the study for two reasons. Firstly to observe how bail reports were actually used in court and secondly to collect data not accessible from other sources but necessary for evaluative purposes, including the costing of bail services and custodial remands. Data were collected using a brief observation schedule which recorded: the time taken for the case to be processed; whether or not bail was requested, opposed and granted; reasons given for and against the granting of bail by the fiscal, sheriff and defence agent; and whether or not reference was made to the bail information report.

For a limited period of time sheriffs' opinions of the value of bail information in individual cases was collected. During a three month period sheriffs were invited to indicate on a form attached to the bail information report whether or not their decisions regarding the granting of bail would have been different in the absence of verified bail information and were given an opportunity comment on the usefulness of information in individual cases if they so wished.

Analysis of court records was undertaken to examine the trends in the relative use of bail and of custodial remands before and after the introduction of the schemes. Data were collected using specially designed monitoring forms. The information sought included: the outcome of the hearing; the type of main offence; the number of charges; the existence or otherwise of charges under the Bail Act; the nature of the appearance; and details relating to the accused (such as age and gender).

Using information derived from bail information worksheets supplemented by data provided by the Scottish Criminal Record Office, a comparison was made of the bail/remand outcomes for accused for whom positive verified information was and was not provided by the bail information schemes.

Bail information and breach of bail

Data provided by the Scottish Criminal Record Office (SCRO) enabled an analysis to be made of the levels of alleged bail abuse among bailees according to whether or not positive verified information may have been a factor in the granting of bail. The SCRO provided data for all bailees who had been interviewed by the schemes over a three month period. The SCRO records were searched approximately six months after the bailees had been interviewed by the bail officers thereby ensuring that most cases had been concluded by the time the search was undertaken. The SCRO data also enabled the factors associated with an increased risk of alleged bail abuse to be identified and a typology of risk to be developed.

Impact on sentencing

Using data provided by SCRO for accused persons interviewed by bail officers over a three month period the influence of bail information on the final outcome of cases (and particularly on the levels of custodial as opposed to non custodial sentencing) was examined by comparing the sentences subsequently received by bailees and by accused who were remanded in custody at first appearance.

Accommodation

Details of accommodation provided and of accommodation providers' experiences were obtained through semi-structured interviews with accommodation providers and bail officers and through analysis of data collected by the schemes. Information derived from scheme records included: characteristics of referrals (such as age, gender, offence, and nature of current problems); whether or not an offer of accommodation was made; reasons for refusal of accommodation; and outcome of referral (i.e. whether the accused was bailed and/or the place was taken up).

Costing of bail services and custodial remand

The cost implications of the bail experiment were assessed by colleagues in the Personal Social Services Research Unit at Kent University. The costing component of the evaluation focused upon: the direct and indirect costs of the schemes; the differential costs of the two schemes; and the comparative costs of custodial remand and bail services.

The costing methodology included an analysis of time diaries completed by staff during one week, which recorded details of the time spent on various tasks and contact with other professionals or public employees. The different routes through the criminal justice system with and without bail services were identified and their associated costs obtained through an analysis of the accounts of the bail schemes. Calculation of the indirect costs was achieved through analysis of salary scales for relevant officials employed by organisations with which the schemes were in contact.

2 The development of bail services

Introduction

As described in the previous chapter, the Scottish Office invited tenders for the provision, on an experimental basis, of bail services to Scottish courts in late 1989. Lothian and Strathclyde Social Work Departments, both in partnership with SACRO - a national voluntary organisation which provides services to offenders and their families - submitted successful proposals. Two pilot bail information and accommodation schemes became operational during 1991. The Lothian scheme provided pre-trial services to Edinburgh Sheriff Court and the Strathclyde scheme to Glasgow Sheriff Court. The present chapter describes the development and organisation of the schemes and the operation of the bail information service. While reference in made, where relevant, to bail accommodation, this aspect of the service is described and discussed more fully in Chapter Four.

The bail scheme in Edinburgh

The Lothian bail information scheme provided a service to Edinburgh Sheriff Court and was staffed by a bail information officer and a bail accommodation officer. Both were officially employed by SACRO but the bail information officer was seconded to the social work department. The bail officers took up post in January 1991.

The bail information officer, a trained social worker, was located within the social work department's Central Offender Unit (COU) - which is based near the sheriff court - and was line-managed by the senior social worker for that team. The COU also provided cover in the bail officer's absence.

The bail accommodation officer who had experience in accommodation provision for ex-offenders was based at Epworth Halls, a day centre for ex-offenders run by SACRO. He was line-managed initially by the manager of the

23

day centre, but subsequently by a senior development officer appointed in September 1991 and more recently by the national Director of Operations. The provision of cover for the bail accommodation officer was an ongoing problem, which was temporarily resolved through the appointment of the senior development officer who undertook this work.

At regular intervals the bail officers met with their managers in SACRO and the social work department to review the progress of the scheme and discuss issues which had emerged. The scheme also had an advisory group which met on a regular basis and which was made up of representatives from different agencies connected with the bail process.

Aims of the pilot

The aim of the pilot scheme was to establish an information and accommodation service which had the primary objective of reducing the use of custodial remand by increasing the opportunities for bail. As the scheme became operational a second objective gained ascendance, namely to provide information which enhanced the quality of bail decisions made by the court. This shift was largely related to discussions in the advisory group in which the value of both positive and negative verified information to the court was raised. It was intended that the accommodation scheme would be based largely on bed and breakfast provision, with back up from beds in existing hostel facilities.

In August 1991, following approval by the advisory group, the scheme's objectives were extended to include the production of a feasibility study on the potential for bail supervision and consideration of the scope for a co-ordinated approach to the provision of mixed short-term accommodation for bailees.

The development of bail services

The advisory group comprised of social work staff, a sheriff, a representative of the Scottish Office and representatives of the fiscal service, sheriff clerks and defence agents. At its first meeting in August 1990 the group addressed a number issues such as the importance of providing impartial verified and accurate information to the court, the need to find suitable accommodation for accused thought likely to re-offend if granted bail, the necessity of avoiding delays in court proceedings and the manner in which services should be targeted and selected. Discussion also focused upon the issue of accused persons recorded by the police as being of no fixed abode (NFA). Some members of the advisory group were of the opinion that most NFAs were resolved by the time they appeared in court while others believed that accused recorded as being of no fixed abode would be a useful group for the scheme to target.

On the basis of this initial meeting and following discussion with a range of relevant agencies, social work staff prepared an operational plan for the information service. Staff were appointed early in 1991 and the scheme came into operation in February of that year.

Bail information

It was envisaged in the operational plan the bail information officer would begin at 8 am by reading through police records on all accused held in St Leonard's Police Station (a central holding station for most people detained in police custody in Edinburgh). The bail information officer would select those cases in which police requested a seven day remand or advised that a custodial remand was likely. It was suggested that this approach would generate sufficient interviews to occupy the bail information officer until the fiscals were able to provide the names of accused whose bail was actually to be opposed (from 9.15 am onwards). The police provided a room with a telephone for use by the bail information officer within which interviews could be held; they also provided access to relevant information.

In practice there were very few instances in which the police requested a seven day remand and, as a result, the bail information officer had to select accused he thought likely to have their bail opposed and conduct these interviews until names of bail opposed cases became available from the fiscals later in the morning. This necessary change in practice raised the question of whether or not interviews were being accurately targeted.

At 10 am prisoners were transported to the sheriff court and the bail information officer returned to the social work office to verify information provided by accused. This was done largely by telephone although personal visits were made if appropriate and if time permitted. Reports were prepared and taken to the sheriff clerks in readiness for the court which sat (usually) at 12 noon. Clerks then distributed the reports in court.

In April 1991 the advisory group met for the first time since the scheme became operational. At this meeting the bail information officer reported that the scheme was running well, though a small number of accused had appeared suspicious of his role and had refused to participate. Two particular concerns were, however, raised. These centred around the issues of targeting and bail accommodation.

In relation to targeting it was reported that there were usually too many cases in which bail was or was likely to be opposed for all to be interviewed by the bail information officer. This was especially true on Mondays when the custody court dealt with all weekend detainees. The bail information officer had to select cases he judged likely to have their bail opposed until the fiscals were in a position to provide names. This was made more difficult because of the limited information available from police files. For example, the bail information officer rarely had access to details of previous convictions (including breach of a current or previous bail order) and in some cases (such as those involving outstanding warrants) records might not even indicate the offence with which the accused had originally been charged. Drawing upon the information available the bail information officer gave priority to cases in which the accused was recorded as being of no fixed address or was likely to require alternative accommodation (in cases involving domestic violence for example). Cases were excluded if the bail information officer was aware that there were no current or previous breaches of bail or if the case was likely to be heard at the District Court. Accused persons thought to be at high risk of a remand in custody were those facing particularly serious charges and those who were identified as having a lengthy criminal record with several pages of previous convictions. Even if the prospect of the accused being granted bail appeared slight the bail information officer would, if time permitted, attempt to verify positive information that might be pertinent to the bail decision.

In practice, little could be done to overcome this problem though the bail information officer reported, over time, that his ability to target interviews had improved. Increasingly, it was said, interviewees seen before names were available from the fiscal were subsequently found to have the granting of bail opposed.

The second issue raised by the bail information officer at the advisory group meeting concerned accommodation referrals. At this stage the only accommodation available to bailees was in probation hostels. Not only was the availability of bail beds (two) very limited, but few accused had been identified as requiring the level of support offered by hostel provision. On the other hand, problems had been encountered when attempting to locate accommodation for accused persons with special needs, such as those with mental health or alcohol-related problems. Hostels which provided specifically for these groups would offer places to bailees after conducting their own assessments but were unwilling to accept same day referrals.

At the advisory group meeting in April 1991 the bail information and accommodation officers both commented that there had been a number of occasions on which hostel places had been obtained but the court had subsequently bailed the accused to another address. Particular concerns were expressed in relation to cases involving domestic violence in which, despite the availability of an alternative verified address, the accused was allowed to return home.

26

By the summer of 1991 the bail information officer reported that targeting had further improved, resulting in a drop in the numbers of interviews conducted and reports prepared. Few accused refused to be interviewed and there had been a growth in the number of requests for verified information from fiscals and defence agents. Arrangements for cover (provided by social workers in the Central Offenders Unit) were said to be working well.

At the advisory group meeting held in the summer of 1991 the bail information officer requested guidance on whether or not negative information (i.e. information likely to reduce the accused person's likelihood of obtaining bail) should be included in bail information reports. In the first few months of operation reports had only been submitted if positive information had been verified (as was the case in the Glasgow scheme and most English bail information schemes). Advisory group members were of the opinion that because the scheme aimed to enhance the quality of information upon which bail decisions were based, both positive and negative information should be submitted. It was consequently agreed that a bail information report would be submitted in all cases, even if no information had been verified or if the information verified was negative in nature and, as such, potentially prejudicial to the accused.

One year into operation the bail information service was said to be working well. Relationships with police, with court-based staff and with other relevant agencies were reported to be good and a number of procedural issues had been resolved. The bail information officer had contacted defence agents to raise awareness of the scheme and to encourage them to refer second appearance cases. Accommodation-related problems had decreased as a result both of a drop in the number of accommodation referrals and an increase in the number of available beds.

By the summer of 1992 the information scheme was still reported to be functioning well and there had been an increase in the number of requests for verbal reports of address checks (from fiscals and defence agents in particular). The main area of concern for the bail information officer related to the circulation of bail information reports. The advisory group agreed to take steps to ensure that reports were always made available in court.

The issue of bail supervision was raised at all advisory group meetings, often in relation to the availability of accommodation. Even before the scheme became operational it was suggested that accommodation should be made available for accused for whom an element of supervision was required to reduce the likelihood of offending on bail.

An objective of the project was to explore the feasibility of bail supervision but advisory group members appeared to hold different interpretations of what bail supervision might involve: should it focus on the provision of support for bailees or should it be more clearly concerned with ensuring that accused persons complied with bail conditions? Neither was it clear who should be responsible for bail supervision. Although in job descriptions and policy documents this function was ascribed to the bail information officer, the advisory group also identified a potential role for the bail accommodation officer by virtue of his regular contact with accommodation providers.

In practice support was available for bailees on a voluntary basis through the bail accommodation officer and accommodation providers. Moreover, if an accused person absconded from bail accommodation, the bail accommodation officer informed the bail information officer who was then able to notify the court thereby providing, in effect, an element of supervision.

The implications of providing supervision of bailees were not fully explored or resolved since staff were fully occupied with operating and developing the information and accommodation services. The bail information officer had contacted a number of bail support/supervision schemes for juveniles in England and Wales and, as a result, had been able to outline some potential problems for the advisory group. At the conclusion of the evaluation discussion of the scope for bail supervision was continuing.

Further development of the bail information scheme

Two possibilities for further development were under discussion towards the end of the evaluation, both of which involved widening the base of referrals. First, the bail information officer had attempted to increase the number of referrals from the courts and from defence agents through the production of publicity material and through contact with defence agents to inform them about the scheme. These approaches had some limited success but further contacts were planned. Second, the scheme aimed to increase the number of interviews with accused persons facing a second appearance. The advisory group agreed that the bail information officer should liaise with prison-based social workers in order to identify appropriate second appearance cases.

The bail scheme in Glasgow

The Glasgow bail scheme was developed on the basis of a series of meetings of a working group comprising fiscals, sheriff clerks and social work staff and of subgroups which were formed to address specific issues. The working group had available to it material provided by the research section of the social work department which had been derived from monitoring of the work of the courts and observation of the courts and of fiscals' marking practice. It prepared outlines of the aims, procedures and practice of the service prior to the appointment of staff to the scheme in August 1991. The two bail officers and a part time assistant who provided clerical support were employed by the social work department. The bail service became operational in October 1991.

The fiscals had a central role in the development of the scheme. Despite initial reservations (Did the introduction of the scheme imply a general criticism of the way in which cases were marked? Would the incidence of bail abuse increase?) fiscals were fully involved in the planning process.

The organisation and management of bail services

The bail officers were members of the social work team covering the courts in Glasgow. Unlike Edinburgh, there was no division of roles between the two staff and each undertook a range of tasks associated with the provision of an information and accommodation service to the courts. The bail officers were managed by the Assistant District Officer (courts) from the social work department and the principal officer for SACRO (Strathclyde). In practice most day to day management was undertaken by the Assistant District Officer but there were regular meetings between him, the bail officers and the principal officer at SACRO to examine the operation and progress of the scheme. The scheme was also overseen by a monitoring and advisory group, comprised, as in Edinburgh, of representatives of agencies involved in the bail process. Whilst it did not have a management function, this group met regularly to review progress and to resolve issues or problems which arose.

The aim of the pilot scheme was to reduce the number of custodial remands (in appropriate cases) by providing verified factual information to the fiscal and defence agents. In practice sheriffs also received copies of bail information reports. Where necessary bail officers also attempted to arrange alternative accommodation for accused.

Bail information

Accused persons detained overnight in police custody were transported to the sheriff court and held there until the court diet at 2 pm. Each day the police compiled a telex containing details of all accused held in custody. A copy of the telex was made available to the bail officers and provided the basis for an initial selection of likely cases. The scheme initially excluded accused who were wanted by another police force (and who would likely be detained regardless of the outcome of the court appearance) as well as petition cases, accused who were thought to have mental health problems and, if insufficient time was available, accused with particularly extensive criminal histories as evidenced by several pages of previous convictions. In court the bail officers could offer immediate confirmation of an address if the telex indicated it had been successfully checked by the police. Under these circumstances a further remand in custody or a recall for an address check was usually avoided.

As cases were marked the fiscal contacted the bail scheme directly to refer those in which bail was to be opposed or in which an address was required. They often provided the reasons for opposition and indicated other relevant concerns. Initially fiscals contacted the scheme only if there were doubts concerning the appropriateness of bail which could be addressed by the provision of additional verified information. In practice however, the bail officers had been able to identify in court a number of cases which could usefully have been referred to the scheme. Following discussion of this issue by the monitoring and advisory group the fiscals agreed that in future all cases in which bail was being opposed would be referred.

Referrals from the fiscals usually became available from 9.15 am onwards. As referrals were made the bail officers interviewed the individuals concerned. An early concern was that the bail officers would have insufficient time to interview all accused persons for whom the granting of bail was being opposed but in practice this was rarely a problem. If cases did have to be selected, accused of no fixed abode were given priority and those cases in which bail was being opposed on the basis of criminal history (particularly if several previous breaches of bail were involved) were accorded lowest priority by the scheme.

Accused were interviewed in police cells. As in Edinburgh, the bail information officer clearly explained the purpose of the interview, obtained the accused person's consent and did not enter into discussion of the alleged offence. After interview, the bail officers attempted to verify information provided by accused. Most verification was attempted by telephone, but visits might be undertaken where this was not possible. Bail information reports were prepared and taken into court by the bail officers shortly before the court sat at 2 pm. At least one bail officer was available in court to distribute reports, deal with queries, pick up any referrals which arose during the session and record the outcomes of cases (including those which might usefully have been referred to the scheme). In the early days of the scheme the bail officers accompanied clients to hostels but this occasionally resulted in neither bail officer being available in court and with the agreement of the advisory group this practice was stopped. Reports were circulated to the sheriff clerks, the fiscal and defence agents. If bail was opposed sheriffs were informed that a bail information report was available.

Referrals initiated by sheriffs were accepted by the scheme. Whilst there was a general policy that only reports containing positive information would be submitted, an exception was made in the event of a specific type of information being requested in court. In these circumstances information would be provided regardless of whether it was likely to increase or decrease the likelihood of the accused person being granted bail. The scheme also accepted a few referrals from defence agents but in order to avoid inappropriate referrals (through, for example, cases being referred even though bail was not opposed) and to maintain the credibility of the scheme it was agreed that defence agents could refer cases only through the procurator fiscal. Occasionally the bail officers also dealt with accused who were already in custody, including those facing second appearances.

By the summer of 1992 the bail information service was regarded by different agencies as providing a credible and worthwhile service. Any problems which arose were addressed through initial discussion with the Assistant District Officer (Courts) who then dealt with the matter informally with the agency concerned and/or raised the issue at the monitoring and advisory group. Regular meetings between the bail officers and the marking teams had also helped to ensure that for the most part all cases in which bail information might be relevant to the bail decision were referred to the scheme.

On an immediately practical level difficulties were encountered when one bail officer was on sick leave for some time and the remaining bail officer found it difficult to sustain the service single-handed. It was agreed that a social work assistant should be trained to undertake some of the work when cover was required.

Further development of the bail information service

There were no concrete plans to extend the remit of the scheme on a formal basis though referrals involving petition cases, requests for interim liberation and means enquiries were occasionally dealt with. Some initial discussion had taken place concerning the extension of the scheme to the district court if the pilot proved successful but this option had not been fully pursued.

Summary

The two schemes were run and organised in different ways. In Edinburgh the information and accommodation functions were undertaken by separate staff based in different locations. The bail information officer was a trained social worker and the bail accommodation officer had worked previously in offender-accommodation. In Glasgow, bail information and accommodation tasks were shared by two bail officers who were not social work trained. Research into four English schemes (Lloyd, 1992) highlighted the benefits and drawbacks of using qualified probation officers in bail schemes. Probation officers were experienced in court work and trained to exercise professional judgement. On the other hand, unqualified staff could perform the relevant tasks equally well, were cheaper to employ and found the job more rewarding. The ability to develop a good rapport with staff in other agencies and interviewing skills were more important than a social work qualification per se. In the Scottish schemes there appeared to be no particular benefits or drawbacks to be derived from the use of trained social work staff. Most of the preparatory work was undertaken by senior social work and SACRO personnel and all the bail staff showed themselves capable of undertaking court-based work and liaison with other agencies and dealing with problems as they emerged.

There were benefits attached to the fact that the bail scheme in Glasgow was located within a well-established court-based social work team which had good operational links with other criminal justice agencies involved in the bail process. The closeness of working relationships between different agencies was reflected in the advisory groups. In Glasgow advisory group meetings were regularly and well attended by members of the different agencies concerned while the sporadic attendance of some agencies in Edinburgh meant that discussion of issues was sometimes delayed.

The separation of the information and accommodation functions created difficulties for the scheme in Edinburgh. The ability of bail staff in Glasgow were to move between information and accommodation roles made it easier for the bail officers to manage their time and to ensure a regular presence in the courts. The bail information officer in Edinburgh, on the other hand, was less well placed to be present in court on a regular basis and this may have prevented the service from achieving the profile and level of acceptance which was evident in Glasgow.

There were, in addition, a number of practical problems related to selection of cases for bail information in Edinburgh. Fiscals in Glasgow were able to refer bail-opposed cases to the scheme as they were marked. The earlier sitting on the custody court in Edinburgh, however, meant that the bail information officer had to anticipate in advance in which cases the fiscal was likely to oppose the granting of bail and often had to do so on the basis of limited information from police reports. Though the bail information officer believed that the targeting of cases had improved with experience, the practical arrangements which prevailed may, as the following chapters suggest, have prevented the scheme from being more effective in diverting accused persons from custodial remands and may, indeed, have resulted in a degree of net-widening in Edinburgh.

3 Bail information

Introduction

The bail information scheme in Edinburgh was monitored for nine months, from 1st May 1991 until the end of January 1992. During that period the bail officer interviewed 553 accused persons and submitted 440 bail information reports (80 per cent of interviews). Most accused were interviewed in the cells at the police station though 15 interviews took place in the sheriff court and one was conducted in prison. In 319 cases (58 per cent of interviews) the fiscal was known to be opposed to the granting of bail. Information on the fiscal's attitude to bail was not available to the bail information officer in 222 cases (40 per cent). Similarly, in most instances the bail information officer was unaware whether bail was subsequently requested by the accused.

The Glasgow scheme was monitored from the 1st November 1991 until the end of March 1992. During that time bail officers were notified that bail was to be opposed or that verified information was required in 418 cases. In most instances (91 per cent) the fiscal had informed the bail officers directly that the granting of bail was to be opposed. A further seven per cent of cases had been referred by the sheriff in court and two per cent were referrals from defence agents. Written bail information reports were submitted in 285 cases (68 per cent) and verbal reports were made in a further five cases. This figure is lower than in Edinburgh because of the different policies adopted with respect to the non-submission of reports. In Glasgow, unlike Edinburgh, reports were generally not submitted unless positive verified information could be provided.

Some of the data presented in this chapter (such as number of previous convictions, current bail status and nature of previous social work involvement) were based upon information provided by accused and their accuracy cannot readily be determined. For instance, observation of interviews conducted by bail officers suggested that accused were sometimes unsure whether or not a bail order was currently in force. It is also possible that some accused attempted to conceal the fact that they were on bail in the hope of increasing

33

their chances of being granted bail on this occasion. However the bail officers were able, in most instances, to verify the information provided by accused and believed that rarely were they deliberately misled by interviewees.

Information about the operation of the Edinburgh and Glasgow schemes is not always directly comparable. This reflects differences between the schemes in terms of the procedures they adopted and the types of information they collected.

Characteristics of accused

In Edinburgh, 89 per cent of the accused who were interviewed by the bail information officer were male. Sixty-one per cent of the 459 for whom data were available (335 cases) were single or separated. Twenty-one per cent of the 530 accused for whom the relevant data were available were of no fixed abode and six per cent) lived outwith Lothian Region. Over half of all accused (55 per cent) were aged 24 years or younger.

Information about the appearance for which the accused was interviewed was often missing. Only two cases were recorded as second appearances. From discussions with the bail information officer it seems likely that the majority of cases in which the type of appearance was unknown involved first appearances.

Most accused in Glasgow were similarly young, single, unemployed men. Over half the accused were 24 years old or less; 97 per cent were male; and 61 per cent were single (with a further 15 per cent divorced or separated). Of the 366 cases for which information was available, 78 per cent were said to be unemployed and the remainder were either in employment or training. A third were recorded as having no fixed address and 62 per cent as being resident in the Glasgow area.

Problems experienced by accused

In interview, the bail officers attempted to identify any personal problems experienced by accused. These are summarised in Table 3.1. Just under half the accused in both schemes indicated that they had no immediate personal problems while around a quarter reported difficulties related to the misuse of drugs. A similar proportion of accused in Edinburgh indicated that they had problems with physical health. Accused in Glasgow, on the other hand, were more likely than those in Edinburgh to have problems related to alcohol abuse. 'Nervous debility' and anxiety were the types of mental health problems most commonly referred to by accused.

34

Table 3.1
Problems reported by accused persons

	Edinburgh (n=491)	Glasgow (n=413)
None	228 (46%)	204 (49%)
Drugs	117 (24%)	111 (27%)
Physical health	115 (23%)	50 (12%)
Alcohol	71 (14%)	91 (22%)
Mental health	22 (4%)	25 (6%)
Other	15 (3%)	5 (1%)

Social work involvement

Accused were asked by bail staff to indicate whether they were currently or had previously been subject to contact with the social work department and, where relevant, the reasons for that contact. The relevant data are summarised in Table 3.2.

Table 3.2
Current and previous social work involvement

	Edinburgh (n=502)	Glasgow (n=361)
Community service/probation	182 (36%)	68 (19%)
Social enquiry report	41 (8%)	44 (12%)
Other offending related supervision	16 (3%)	19 (5%)
Childcare/supervision	14 (3%)	31 (9%)
Unspecified	76 (15%)	69 (19%)
Other*	45 (9%)	46 (12%)
None	128 (25%)	84 (23%)

* Voluntary contact, family, drug and alcohol problems and hospital social work

Around three-quarters of the accused in both schemes had some current or previous social work involvement. Just under half the accused in Edinburgh and more than a third of those in Glasgow had been in contact with the social work department in relation to adult offending. A third of accused in Edinburgh (168 accused) were current social work clients while this was true of 31 per cent of accused in Glasgow (111 accused).

Offence-related variables

Seventy-nine per cent of accused in Edinburgh were recorded as facing a new charge and over half (53 per cent) were alleged to be in breach of bail. One in six accused had been brought in on warrants, most of which were non-appearance warrants or straight apprehension warrants.

When questioned about their bail status by the bail information officer, just over half the accused in Edinburgh (53 per cent) maintained they were not currently on bail. A significant majority (85 per cent) indicated they had been arrested before and most (77 per cent) admitted to having one or more previous convictions. Accused had difficulty estimating exactly how many previous convictions they had. Fifteen per cent claimed to have one previous conviction; 21 per cent estimated they had between one and three previous convictions; 29 per cent said they had between four and nine; and the remainder had more than nine). Just under a third of accused (32 per cent) admitted that they had failed to appear in court in the past.

Table 3.3 shows the types of offences with which accused in Edinburgh had been charged. Details of offences were available for only 426 accused, many of whom were facing multiple charges. The bail information officer extracted information from police files and details of the charges in warrant cases were often not available. Scheme policy, moreover, prohibited the bail information officer from discussing the current alleged offence with accused persons.

As Table 3.3 indicates, accused had most commonly been charged with committing offences involving dishonesty, such as thefts and housebreakings. A third had been charged in connection with offences involving violence, primarily common assaults.

Table 3.3
Charges faced by accused in Edinburgh

	Number of accused (n=426)	% of accused
Dishonesty	266	62
Public order	172	40
Violence	151	35
Criminal justice	40	9
Road traffic	38	9
Drugs	30	7
Firearms/explosives	7	2
Sexual	2	1
Other [*]	15	4

[*] Includes abduction, Litter Act and other miscellaneous offences

In Glasgow data regarding current bail status were provided by the fiscals in 376 cases. No breach of bail was alleged in 60 per cent of these cases. Three-quarters of the remainder were alleged to be in breach of a single bail order while a quarter had more than one breach of bail recorded. Fewer than one in ten accused (eight per cent) claimed to have no previous convictions. By contrast, more than half the accused (54 per cent) indicated that they had previously been convicted on nine or more occasions.

In 380 of the 397 cases for which relevant details were available accused in Glasgow were alleged to have committed a new offence. In 376 cases details of the main charge were available and these are summarised in Table 3.4. It should be noted bail scheme practice regarding the recording of charges differed between Glasgow and Edinburgh. Whereas all charges were recorded in Edinburgh, the staff in Glasgow recorded only the main charge faced by the accused.

Over half of the accused had been charged with dishonesty offences, the most common offence being housebreaking. Just over a fifth were alleged to have committed offences involving violence (mainly assaults) and 12 per cent had been charged with public order offences (mainly breaches of the peace).

Table 3.4
Main charge faced by accused in Glasgow

	Number of accused (n=376)	% of accused
Dishonesty	202	54
Violence	80	21
Public order	44	12
Road traffic	20	5
Drugs	12	3
Firearms/explosives	3	1
Criminal justice	3	1
Sexual	2	1
Other*	10	3

* Includes abduction, matrimonial homes and other miscellaneous offences

First and second appearances

The bail officers in Glasgow, unlike their counterpart in Edinburgh, dealt with a number of cases involving second appearances. A total of 336 cases (83 per cent) involved first appearances and 82 (16 per cent) second appearances. The small number of remaining cases included bail applications and reductions to summary. Second appearances were more likely to involve solemn proceedings (37 per cent compared with 11 per cent of first appearance cases). Over half of the second appearance cases (51 per cent) had previously been remanded in custody and just over a third (35 per cent) had been continued without plea at first appearance. Second appearances were more likely to have been referred by the sheriff, less likely to be current social work clients and less likely to be allegedly in breach of bail. A third of second appearance cases were referred for accommodation to be checked.

Identifying and verifying information in Edinburgh

The types of information offered by the accused for verification by the bail information officer in Edinburgh are summarised in Table 3.5.

Table 3.5
Information offered for verification by accused in Edinburgh

	No. of accused (n=543)	% of accused
Accommodation	408	75
Employment/training	184	34
Problems (unspecified)	34	6
Drug/alcohol problem	29	5
Family situation	14	3
Health	3	1
Social work contact	3	1
Other	3	1

Accommodation was most often offered for verification by accused, followed by information on employment, education or training. The types of information offered in cases where reports were and were not submitted were very similar.

Table 3.6
Sources of verification identified by accused

	Number of accused (n=543)	% of accused
Parents	150	34
Employer	104	19
Partner/ex-partner	79	14
Other family member	71	13
Health workers	53	9
Accommodation providers	18	3
Social work department	4	1
DSS	1	0
Other	76	14
Not known	22	4

Accused additionally offered suggestions to the bail information officer as regards individuals or agencies who might serve as sources of verification for the information provided. Table 3.6 summarises the potential sources of verification suggested by accused persons. In some cases several potential sources of verification were put forward by accused.

As Table 3.6 indicates, parents, other family members and employers were the most common sources of verification proposed by accused persons. Public sector agencies, on the other hand, were rarely suggested. 'Other' sources identified by accused persons included friends and flatmates, clergy and Alcoholics Anonymous. There were no apparent differences between the cases in which reports were submitted and those in which they were not.

In 113 cases (20 per cent of all interview) no bail information report was submitted to the court. Table 3.7 summarises the reasons for non-submission of reports.

Table 3.7
Reasons why no report was submitted

	Number of reports (n=113)	% of reports
Unable to verify information	37	33
No verification attempted	16	14
Unable to verify accommodation	9	8
Bail not an issue	7	6
Accused declined	7	6
Case went to district court	7	6
Lack of time	3	3
No accommodation available	2	2
No useful information	1	1
No positive information	1	1
No explanation	23	21

The main reason for non-submission of a report was the bail information officer's inability to verify any information provided by the accused. This could occur if he had been unable to contact the sources of verification identified by the accused. In 16 cases the bail information officer had, for various reasons, not attempted to verify information. This occurred, for example, if information about the fiscal's attitude to bail was unavailable and other cases were, as a consequence, accorded higher priority. In a number of cases reports were not submitted because they fell outwith the remit of the scheme (for example, bail was not opposed or the case was subsequently dealt with in the district court). Some, though not all, of these cases involved accused persons who were interviewed before the bail information officer had received an indication from the fiscal of those cases in which bail was being opposed.

In one instance a report was not submitted because there was no positive information to convey. This occurred before the scheme introduced a policy of submitting a report regardless of whether no information or only negative information had been verified.

Table 3.8 shows the different types of information contained in bail information reports.

Table 3.8
Information contained in bail information reports

	Number of reports (n=440)	% of reports
Accommodation	356	81
None verified	105	24
Employment/training	93	21
Social work contact	89	20
Drugs/alcohol	29	7
Health	16	4
Family commitments	10	2
Help available	10	2
Community support	5	1
Mental health	5	1
Problems (unspecified)	5	1
Other positive information	7	2
Negative information	12	3

Bail information reports focused primarily on accommodation, mainly confirming that the accused had an address to which she or he was able to return. Table 3.9 indicates the sources of verified information contained in bail information reports. Social work personnel constituted over a third of the sources contacted. Family members (usually parents) were the next largest group who were contacted to verify information provided by accused to the bail information officer.

Comparing information provided and information checked, it was found that the bail information officer was able to verify contact with agencies such as social work departments and drugs projects on most occasions. Information about employment was only verified in around half the cases in which it was offered for verification by accused. Family members proved particularly difficult to contact. Some were not contactable by telephone while others were not at home when the bail information officer attempted to make contact with them (often they were making their way to court).

Table 3.9
Sources of information cited in bail information reports

	Number of reports (n=440)	% of reports
Social work department	162	37
Parents	66	15
Other family	43	10
Employer	37	8
Health agencies	33	8
Friend/neighbour	30	7
Partner/ex partner	21	5
Accommodation agencies	19	4
Bail accommodation officer	15	3
Police	14	3
Other*	12	3
Unable to contact source	39	9

* Includes minister, counsellor, co-accused etc.

Initially bail reports were only submitted in Edinburgh when positive information had been verified. After a few months of operation it became agreed policy to submit a bail information report in all cases, regardless of whether or not information had been verified and regardless of whether or not information that had been verified might be disadvantageous to the accused.

In practice, however, the vast majority of reports (83 per cent) contained exclusively positive information. In a further 13 per cent of reports none of the

42

information provided by the accused had been verified by the bail information officer. Three per cent of reports contained both positive and negative information and only one per cent contained exclusively negative information. The information contained in two per cent of reports could not readily be classified as positive or negative.

Identifying and verifying information in Glasgow

The types of information offered by accused for verification by the bail officers in Glasgow are summarised in Table 3.10.

Table 3.10
Information offered for verification by accused

	Number of accused (n=353)	% of accused
Accommodation	310	88
Drug/alcohol problem*	49	14
Employment/training	49	14
Health	39	11
Progress on probation	22	6
Family situation	17	4
Social work contact	15	5
Mental health	13	4
Progress on community service	12	3
Benefits	7	2
Other	7	2
Not specified	6	2

* Includes verification that the accused had a problem and/or that accused was seeking or receiving help or treatment

In almost 90 per cent of cases accused persons suggested that the bail officers attempt to verify that they had an address to return to if released by the court. This usually involved the bail officers verifying that the accused lived with her or his family or had her or his own tenancy. In 98 cases, however, the bail officers attempted to find alternative accommodation for an accused person. Other types of information to be investigated included the existence of drug or alcohol problems, employment status and health.

It is evident from Table 3.11 that a wide range of organisations and individuals were identified by the accused and by the bail officers as potential sources of verification of information provided by the former. Accused generally suggested family members (mainly parents) and friends as the main sources of verification. Accommodation agencies (mainly hostels) were identified where appropriate and more usually by bail officers. In approximately a quarter of cases social work staff were considered likely sources of verification and in a further 16 per cent of cases health agencies - GPs and hospital staff - were identified.

Table 3.11
Sources of verification identified by accused and bail officers

	Number of accused (n=346)	% of accused
Parents	109	33
Accommodation agencies[1]	90	26
Social work department	78	23
Other family	77	22
Health agencies	56	16
Partner	35	10
Friend/neighbour	33	10
Drugs projects	33	10
Employer	28	8
Police	19	5
DSS	13	4
Other agencies[2]	17	5

[1] Hostels and the housing department

[2] Includes solicitors, estate agents

A total of 290 bail reports were submitted to the court, including five verbal reports for which worksheets were not completed. Table 3.12 summarises the types of information contained in the 285 written reports.

Table 3.12
Information contained in the bail information reports

	Number of reports (n=285)	% of reports
Accommodation	220	77
Drug/alcohol problems	33	12
Social work contact	30	11
Health	26	9
Other positive information	13	5
Employment/training	12	4
Family commitments	10	4
Mental health	7	2
Unverified	37	13

In around three-quarters of reports the bail officers provided verified information concerning the accused person's accommodation status. In just over half of these cases the accused was able to return to the family home or to his or her own tenancy. In three-tenths of cases a hostel place was located for the accused and in a sixth of cases where information regarding accommodation was verified the bail officers had located alternative accommodation (with, for example, other family members) for the accused. In 30 cases (11 per cent of reports) the bail officers were able to verify that the accused was making satisfactory progress on an existing probation or community service order. In 37 other cases the bail officers had been unable to verify any information provided by the accused. In eight of these cases alternative accommodation had been sought for the accused but had not been found.

Table 3.13 summarises the sources of verified information contained in the bail reports. In three-quarters of cases the bail officers relied upon public sector agencies to provide verified information. Hostels and the social work department were the main sources of verification.

45

Table 3.13
Sources of information cited in bail information reports

	Number of reports (n=281)	% of reports
Accommodation providers[1]	91	32
Parents	59	21
Social work department	48	17
Other Family	44	15
Health agencies	29	10
Drug rehab/treatment	24	8
Friend/neighbour	20	7
Partner	19	7
Police	12	4
DSS	10	4
Employer	8	3
Job centre etc	4	1
Other[2]	7	2

[1] Includes hostels and housing department

[2] Includes estate agent, landlady

Reports were generally only submitted in Glasgow if the information contained therein was likely to enhance the accused person's chances of being granted bail. The exception involved cases which were referred to the scheme directly by the courts with an attendant request that specific types of information be checked by the bail officers. In all but one of the cases referred by a sheriff a report was submitted to the court.

In a total of 128 cases (31 per cent of referrals) no written or verbal report was submitted. Ninety seven per cent of these cases had been referred by the procurator fiscal. The reasons for non-submission of reports are summarised in Table 3.14. In thirty eight per cent of cases accused persons had not been able to provide the bail officers with information which, if verified, would be likely to increase their chances of obtaining bail. In a further 16 per cent of cases the bail officers had been unable to verify information offered by the accused. In 20 cases no bail information report was submitted because negative information alone had been verified.

Table 3.14
Reasons why no report was submitted

	Number of reports (n=128)	% of reports
No useful information	49	38
No positive information	20	16
Unable to verify information	16	13
Bail not an issue[1]	16	13
No explanation given	14	11
Accused declined assistance	4	3
Address check only	4	3
DA/relative verified	3	2
Other[2]	2	2

[1] Includes client in custody, bail not requested or bail not available

[2] Includes no time to verify and client ill

Accused for whom reports were not submitted were less likely to be of no fixed abode (12 per cent compared with 44 per cent of those for whom bail information reports were available). They were also less likely to be represented by the duty solicitor (seven per cent compared with 16 per cent of those for whom reports were available).

The outcome of cases in Edinburgh

Table 3.15 shows the outcomes at first appearance for all accused interviewed by the bail information officer (excluding 78 cases in which the relevant information was unavailable) while Table 3.16 summarises the outcomes of cases according to the type of information provided.

Clearly there was little difference in outcome according to whether reports contained positive or other types of information, though accused for whom reports were submitted containing positive information were more likely to have been granted bail with standard conditions and less likely to be given bail orders with special conditions attached.

Table 3.15
Outcome at first appearance

	Number of accused (n=475)	% of accused
Standard bail	188	40
Special bail	53	11
Remand in custody	149	31
Ordained	25	5
Convicted	56	12
Other	4	1

Table 3.16
Outcome by type of information in bail report

	Positive (n=286)	Other* (n=60)
Standard bail	130 (45%)	23 (38%)
Special bail	34 (12%)	10 (17%)
Remand in custody	101 (35%)	22 (37%)
Ordained	17 (6%)	2 (3%)
Other	4 (1%)	3 (5%)

* Reports containing negative, no or mixed information.

It will be recalled that in the Edinburgh scheme the bail information officer began interviewing accused in police custody prior to receiving the full list of opposed cases from the fiscal. This procedure was necessary to ensure that as many interviews as possible could be completed before accused were taken to court. Until he was informed of those cases in which the Crown was opposed to the granting of bail, the bail information officer interviewed those accused for whom it was thought unlikely that the fiscal would have a favourable attitude towards bail. A variety of criteria, such as the absence of a fixed address, previous convictions and bail history, were taken into consideration in identifying cases in which bail was likely to be opposed. The question therefore arises as to how accurate this method of targeting by the bail information officer was.

Fiscal attitudes towards bail, and the reasons for opposition where appropriate, were not always known by the bail information officer and recorded on the bail worksheet. However, to enable the issue of targeting to be addressed, the procurators fiscal in Edinburgh provided the researchers with a list of all cases in which bail was opposed during a four-week period in December 1991 and January 1992. By matching these cases with the data collected from bail information worksheets during the same period, the accuracy of targeting could be assessed.

The fiscal opposed bail for 93 accused persons during this period. In the same four weeks 48 accused were interviewed by the bail information officer, 38 of whom were individuals for whom bail was being opposed in the sheriff court. Overall, then, the bail information officer interviewed 41 per cent (38/93) of accused identified by the fiscals as those for whom bail would be opposed while 21 per cent of interviews (10/48) were with accused for whom the fiscal had a favourable attitude towards the granting of bail.

Table 3.17
Fiscal grounds for opposition to bail

Grounds for opposition	Interviewed by bail officer (n=28)	Not interviewed by bail officer (n=30)	Total (n=58)
Previous convictions/record	13	10	23
NFA/address	11	9	20
Further enquiries	6	5	11
Previous/current bail offences	4	5	9
'Various'	4	5	9
Nature/seriousness of offence	2	5	7
Failure to appear	1	5	6
Breach of special conditions	1	-	1
Psychiatric reports	-	1	1
Psychiatric history	-	1	1
Current probation	-	1	1
Safety of witness	1	-	1

The reasons for bail being opposed by the Crown were also provided for a total of 58 of the 93 accused and are summarised in Table 3.17. For most accused (40) more than one reason for opposition was provided. The previous criminal history of the accused, for example, was the sole reason for opposition in only six of the 23 cases in which it featured as a reason. Similarly, the nature or seriousness of the offence was cited as the only reason for opposition in 2/7 cases. Surprisingly perhaps, given that address alone was said by fiscals only rarely to be the sole reason for opposing bail, this occurred in 13 of the 20 cases in which address was an issue. In four of these cases, however, the concern was not over the lack of a fixed abode but the suitability of an existing address and possible need for an alternative address to be found.

Overall, there appeared to be little (in terms of reason for fiscal opposition) to differentiate those accused selected for interview by the bail information officer from those who could not be interviewed through lack of time. Accused for whom bail was being opposed on the basis of the nature or seriousness of the offence or because of previous failure to appear were less likely to have been interviewed by the bail information officer. This is consistent with the bail officer's reported prioritisation of cases for interview: when time was limited accused who seemed least likely to be bailed even if positive verified information was provided were accorded the lowest priority for interview by the bail information officer. By matching the reasons for fiscal opposition to the data collected from the bail information worksheets, the grounds for fiscal opposition to bail could be linked to the outcome of cases (Table 3.18).

Table 3.18
Reasons for fiscal opposition by outcome

	Bailees (n=15)	Custodial remands (n=10)
Record	7	6
NFA/Address	8	2
Further enquiries	2	4
Previous/current bail offences	3	1
'Various'	1	1
Nature/seriousness of offence	1	1
Failure to appear	1	-
Breach of special conditions	-	1
Safety of witness	-	1

Three of the 28 accused who were interviewed by the bail information officer and for whom the grounds for fiscal opposition to bail were known pled guilty at first appearance and the subsequent outcomes and disposals were unavailable from the bail worksheets. Fifteen of the remaining accused were bailed and ten were remanded in custody for further enquiries or pending trial.

Accommodation was an issue in ten cases. In each of the six cases where it was the sole concern the accused was granted bail. The accused person's address had been verified in four instances and in another the bail information officer had been able to confirm that the accused was a university student. Two accused for whom there were other grounds for opposition to bail in addition to accommodation were bailed (in one case supported accommodation had been obtained, while in the other the bail information officer had been unable to verify an address). Two others were remanded in custody: in one instance no suitable accommodation could be found and in the other an address provided by a friend of the accused had not been independently verified by the bail information officer.

The record of the accused was an issue in 13 cases, seven of whom were granted bail. An address had been verified for five of these accused, in three cases along with additional verified information (employment, drug treatment and good response to recent probation order). No information was verified in one case and in one other the bail information officer had been unable to verify that the accused had a fixed address, but had confirmed that the accused was currently in employment.

Accommodation had also been verified for five of the six accused who were remanded in custody and for whom previous criminal history was a factor in the fiscal's opposition to bail. In one of the two cases in which address alone had been verified, bail was being opposed as a result of concerns over the safety of witnesses; in the other case, the accused was remanded in custody overnight while further checks were made on the reliability of an address provided by a friend. In two of the three cases where other positive information had been verified in addition to accommodation bail was also being opposed while the case was continued for further enquiries.

The numbers involved are clearly small; however, it does appear that when the bail information officer was able to provide verification of accommodation/and or additional positive information concerning community ties, and bail was being opposed primarily or solely on the basis of accommodation, then bail was likely to be granted by the court.

The outcome of cases in Glasgow

In Glasgow, unlike Edinburgh, almost all referrals to the scheme were known to be cases which the fiscal was opposed to the granting of bail. In some instances the bail officers were aware that fiscal opposition would not be sustained if verified information (such as an address) could be provided. The fiscal was ultimately prepared to agree in court to bail being granted in 34 per cent of cases, in 16 per cent conditionally upon a suitable address being verified. Periods of observation by the researchers in the custody court confirmed that in some instances verified information provided by the bail officers removed the fiscal's opposition to bail while in others information provided in court by the defence agent enabled the fiscal to adopt a favourable attitude towards the granting of bail. The fiscal was less likely to oppose bail at second appearance (39 per cent of cases compared with 62 per cent at first appearance). Fiscal opposition at second appearance centred primarily around concerns regarding accommodation.

The reasons for fiscal opposition to bail were collected from scheme records, having been provided directly to the bail officers by fiscals or obtained by the bail officers in court. Table 3.19 summarises the grounds for fiscal opposition in the 306 cases for which this information was available. It is clear that the fiscal was most commonly opposed to the granting of bail on the basis of the accused person's criminal record. In a quarter of cases the ground for opposition was an alleged breach of a current bail order. In just under half the cases the fiscal opposed bail because of concerns about the accused person's address, usually because he or she was recorded as being of no fixed abode.

Table 3.19
Fiscal grounds for opposition to bail

	Number of accused (n=306)	% of accused
Record	172	56
Address	143	47
Breach of bail	75	25
Other criminal factors[*]	18	6
Mental health	7	2

[*] Includes further enquiries, threat to witnesses, likely to abscond, nature of charges etc.

The outcomes of cases at first and second appearance are shown in Table 3.20. Accused were more likely at first appearance to be remanded in custody and were less likely to be granted bail on standard conditions. Most of the accused making a second appearance had previously been remanded in custody (87 per cent). This is consistent with fiscals' comments that in relatively few cases was a further remand in custody likely at second appearance. None of the sample were ordained to appear at either first or second appearance.

Table 3.20
Outcome at first and second appearance

	First appearance (n=332)	Second appearance (n=82)
Standard bail	122 (37%)	41 (50%)
Special bail	15 (5%)	8 (10%)
Remand in custody	109 (33%)	15 (18%)
Ordained	0 (0%)	0 (0%)
Convicted	81 (24%)	18 (22%)
Liberated	5 (2%)	0 (0%)

Table 3.21 summarises the outcomes at first appearance by the grounds upon which the fiscal was opposed to the granting of bail. Over half of the accused whose bail was opposed on the grounds of address were eventually bailed at first appearance. When bail was opposed because of the accused person's criminal record or alleged breach of bail, accused were more likely to be remanded in custody. When the objection had been on the basis of an unsuitable address, a special condition was often attached to the bail order.

The same data for second appearance cases are summarised in Table 3.22. Data were available for 69 of the 82 accused involved in second appearances. Accused for whom bail was opposed on the grounds of address or concerns about mental health were most likely to be granted bail.

Table 3.21
Outcome at first appearance by grounds for opposition

	Address	Record	Breach of bail	Other criminal[1]	Other[2]
Bail	49 (53%)	39 (26%)	22 (32%)	4 (44%)	3 (50%)
RIC	29 (31%)	86 (57%)	33 (49%)	3 (33%)	1 (17%)
Convicted	5 (5%)	20 (13%)	7 (10%)	2 (22%)	1 (17%)
Other	10 (11%)	7 (5%)	6 (9%)	0 (0%)	1 (17%)
Total	93	152	68	9	6

Grounds for opposition

[1] Includes threat to witnesses and nature of charges
[2] Includes mental health, likely to abscond and drug problem

Table 3.22
Outcome at second appearance by grounds for opposition

	Address	Record	Breach of bail	Other criminal[1]	Other[2]
Bail	34 (69%)	5 (22%)	2 (29%)	2 (33%)	2 (66%)
RIC	11 (22%)	5 (22%)	0 (0%)	4 (66%)	1 (33%)
Convicted	3 (6%)	4 (17%)	1 (14%)	0 (0%)	0 (0%)
Other	1 (2%)	9 (39%)	4 (57%)	0 (0%)	0 (0%)
Total	49	23	7	6	3

Grounds for opposition

[1] Includes threat to witnesses and nature of charges
[2] Mental health

There were, however, differences in the fiscals' attitudes to bail (as recorded by the bail officers in court) between cases in which reports were submitted and those in which they were not. The fiscal was less likely to oppose bail in court if a bail information report was available. Thus bail was opposed in 87 per cent of cases in which no report was submitted compared with only 58 per cent of cases in which a bail information report was made available. All but one of thirteen accused in the latter group (five per cent of cases) were subsequently bailed following an overnight remand to enable an address to be checked by the bail officers.

The outcomes at first appearance for cases in which reports were and were not submitted are summarised in Table 3.23. When bail reports were submitted to the court half the accused were granted bail at first appearance. Fourteen of these accused (six per cent of all those for whom reports were provided) were granted bail on special conditions. Accused for whom reports were not submitted were more likely to be remanded in custody or to plead guilty.

Table 3.23
Outcome at first appearance by availability of a bail information report

	No report (n=107)	Report[*] (n=225)
Bail	23 (22%)	114 (50%)
Remand in custody	43 (40%)	66 (29%)
Convicted	38 (36%)	43 (19%)
Liberated	3 (3%)	2 (1%)
Ordained	0 (0%)	0 (0%)

[*] Includes three verbal reports

Table 3.24 summarises the comparable data for second appearances. At second appearance, as at the first, accused were more likely to be bailed and less likely to be remanded in custody if a bail report containing verified information was submitted to the court.

Table 3.24
Outcome at second appearance by availability
of a bail information report

	No report (n=19)	Report (n=63)
Standard bail	5 (26%)	44 (70%)
Remand in custody	5 (32%)	9 (14%)
Convicted	8 (42%)	10 (16%)
Liberated/ordained	0 (0%)	0 (0%)

Summary

During the period of monitoring, 553 accused were interviewed in Edinburgh and 440 bail information reports were submitted to the court. The staff in Glasgow conducted interviews with 418 accused, submitting 285 written and five verbal reports. In both schemes interviewees were mainly young, unemployed men facing charges for offences involving dishonesty and around a quarter reported having health, alcohol or drugs problems. In Edinburgh a fifth of interviewees were recorded as being of no fixed abode. Three-quarters had had some previous social work involvement, just under a half of whom were current social work clients. The majority of accused faced a new charge (mainly for offences of dishonesty or violence) and over half were alleged to be in breach of bail. Forty per cent on interviewees in Glasgow were alleged to be in breach of bail and a third were of no fixed abode. A quarter claimed to be current social work clients and a further 40 per cent reported having had previous social work involvement, in most instances related to offending.

In both schemes the bail officers attempted to verify information related to accommodation in the majority of cases. Whilst accused persons usually suggested family members (mainly parents) or employers as likely sources of verified information, in practice most verification was through social work department personnel and other public sector agencies. The use of public sector sources to verify information occurred largely because they were easier for bail staff to contact than were the friends or family of the accused. Public sector sources could also verify several pieces of information on the basis of one telephone call. The Edinburgh scheme introduced a policy of submitting a bail information report in all cases though over 80 per cent of reports contained positive information.

Overall, forty per cent of accused in Edinburgh were granted bail on standard conditions and a further 11 per cent were bailed with a special condition attached. Thirty-one per cent were remanded in custody. Data provided by the fiscals suggested that the provision of positive verified information in a bail report was linked to the granting of bail by the court where bail was being opposed primarily on the grounds of accommodation.

The fiscals in Glasgow mainly opposed bail on the basis of the accused person's criminal record or address. When the basis of opposition was criminal record, breach of bail or other concerns relating specifically to the current case, accused were most likely to be remanded in custody. Bail was more likely to be granted if the fiscal was opposed to the granting of bail on the grounds of the lack of a suitable address. When reports were available in Glasgow the fiscal was much less likely to oppose bail and accused were more likely to be granted bail both at first and second appearances.

4 Bail accommodation

Introduction

The previous chapter concentrated upon the bail information service provided by the two schemes. It was also expected, however, that both schemes would endeavour to access accommodation for accused persons who had been detained in police custody where this was required. The arrangements which prevailed in the Edinburgh and Glasgow bail schemes with respect to the provision of accommodation for accused who had been interviewed by the bail officers have been alluded to briefly in Chapter Two. The activities of the bail scheme staff in this regard form the basis of the present chapter.

Bail accommodation in Edinburgh

The bail accommodation officer was appointed early in 1991 and the accommodation scheme became operational in February, shortly after the information scheme. The focus of bail accommodation was intended to be landlady provision supplemented by beds in the two probation hostels. Since hostel beds were immediately available they provided the basis for bail accommodation in the early stages of the scheme while landlady provision was developed. A retainer fund of £8,000 was made available to reimburse any losses to accommodation providers and to keep beds available for the scheme. Until landlady provision became available the bail information officer only referred accused thought suitable for hostel accommodation.

The bail accommodation officer's role involved developing and maintaining landlady accommodation, liaising with hostels, supporting accommodation providers, providing accused persons with information on welfare rights and providing help and support with benefit claims and move-on accommodation.

Hostel provision mainly centred on two units: Albrae, a probation hostel run by Lothian Social Work Department and Allalon, a voluntary sector probation hostel. Albrae accepted women over 16 years old and men aged 20 and over and took referrals from all groups of clients with the exception of those with mental health problems. Allalon provided accommodation for young men aged between 16 and 21 years who had pled guilty to an offence.

After some initial difficulties hostel placements generally worked well. The bail accommodation officer reportedly spent considerable time explaining the bail scheme to hostel staff and developing good working relationships which enabled any concerns staff had about offering places to bailees to be successfully resolved.

By virtue of their unconvicted status, the provision of accommodation to bailees did create practical problems for hostel staff. The fact, for instance, that same-day placement was necessary prevented hostels from conducting their own assessments of bailees. The limited nature of information about individual bailees, and especially the absence of details concerning their criminal histories (whether, for example, they had a history of violent or sexual offences, of fire-rasing or of offences related to the abuse of alcohol or drugs) was also of some concern both to the bail accommodation officer and to hostel staff. The accommodation officer found it necessary to stop accepting potential hostel referrals because he was unable to furnish staff with adequate information about the potential risks likely to be faced by accepting bailees. The matter was initially raised at the advisory group and, following discussions with the bail information and accommodation officers, was satisfactorily resolved through the fiscal agreeing to inform the bail information officer of any relevant details in a bailee's criminal history before the offer of a bed was finalised.

Because the length of residence was unpredictable hostels found it difficult to maintain occupancy levels while ensuring that beds were available for bailees. While some bailees could be resident for very brief periods others could be in residence for periods of up to a year, preventing other client groups, such as probationers, from having access to these beds. Since their levels of traditional referrals fluctuated, hostels had difficulty reserving beds for use by the scheme.

Bailees were, furthermore, said to present special financial problems. Some were not eligible for benefits, others had arrears deducted from a new claim and in other cases there were delays in payments being made. If an accused was in residence only for a brief period claims might not be sorted sufficiently quickly with the result that hostels could suffer financial loss.

Finally, hostel staff were concerned about the possible consequences of convicted residents having regular contact with those on bail. Unconvicted bailees might be at greater risk of further offending if placed with convicted offenders. On a practical level too, their different legal status required that bailees had to be managed differently from other residents.

Despite these concerns, hostel staff and the bail accommodation officer reported good and flexible working relationships. Hostel staff appreciated the work the bail accommodation officer undertook with themselves and with bailees. Most bailees did not have field social workers and the bail accommodation officer fulfilled many of these functions.

The landlady scheme

Hostel provision was intended to provide a back-up to accommodation provided by a network of supported landladies. Although the development of landlady provision was considered to be a priority several matters had to be clarified before recruitment could commence. How should landladies be compensated in the event of accused persons not paying rent and who should be responsible for insurance against any damage or loss incurred? Guidance was sought from the Regional Solicitor but the bail accommodation officer reported that there had been a considerable delay in receiving a response. A further problem concerned the calculation of benefits which for those in landlady placements were made on a weekly basis. To ensure that landladies would be paid in full the bail accommodation officer arranged for placements to landladies offering beds to bailees to be treated on the same basis as hostel payments and calculated on a daily basis.

Shortly before the start of the scheme the environmental health department in Edinburgh introduced new registration procedures for landladies and this was believed to have reduced the pool of available accommodation. The experiences of others working in the supported accommodation field suggested that it would be difficult to recruit landladies to the scheme. The first recruitment campaign began in the spring of 1991 and by the summer of that year only one landlady had been recruited. Following a successful newspaper recruitment campaign there were eight landlady beds available by the beginning of 1992.

Unfortunately there was also at this time a significant drop in the number of referrals for bail accommodation and this made it difficult for the bail accommodation officer to retain landladies who had been recruited to the scheme. In an attempt to maintain bail provision the bail accommodation officer accepted referrals from other clients in addition to bailees and made use of the retainer fund to keep beds available. Landladies were, however, reluctant to keep beds empty even if they were paid. To resolve this difficulty the advisory group agreed that beds could be offered to bailees from other courts in Lothian Region on the condition that priority be given to bailees from Edinburgh Sheriff Court.

Difficulties relating to length of residence (especially lengthy periods of residence which precluded the use of beds by other bailees) and the absence of accurate information about the previous offending histories of bailees, both of which had arisen in relation to hostel placements, were also encountered in connection with landlady provision and subsequently resolved. Despite the progress made by the bail accommodation officer in developing effective working relationships with accommodation providers, resolving a range of practical problems and dealing with a number of placements some more intractable structural difficulties remained.

There was, for example, a critical lack of emergency accommodation in Edinburgh, both for those who simply required somewhere to stay and for those with particular needs, such as bailees with a mental health problems or with significant problems related to the use of alcohol or drugs. Bailees with a history of violent or sexual offending and those who had attempted suicide in the past also proved difficult to place since the bail accommodation officer was reluctant, at least initially, to ask landladies to take on cases as demanding as these.

Landladies continued to prove difficult, though not impossible, to recruit and retain, particularly within the city. In order to ensure that some landlady beds were available even during periods of low levels of referrals, the retainer fund was eventually used to reserve one or two beds for the bail scheme.

Finally the bail accommodation officer identified several other factors which he believed had served to impede the development of the bail accommodation service. The day centre in which he was based was sometimes closed at times when the bail accommodation officer had to be available to the courts, there was a lack of dedicated administrative support and obtaining cover for periods of leave had proved problematic. Because of broader changes within the organisation, the level of management guidance and support provided to the bail accommodation officer was less than adequate. These latter difficulties were alleviated when the senior development officer came into post.

The bail accommodation officer was also of the opinion that bail accommodation had tended to be accorded less importance than the information aspect of the scheme. This was reflected, for example, in the absence of accommodation providers on the advisory group and the in lack of policy and practice guidelines for the development of accommodation for bailees.

The bail accommodation officer in Edinburgh recorded details of

61

accommodation referrals and monitored progress and outcome. During the nine month period during which the scheme was monitored by the authors 62 referrals were made to the bail accommodation scheme.

Characteristics of accused

Most of the accused referred for accommodation were male (92 per cent) and single (66 per cent). Forty eight per cent were aged 24 or under. Eighty four per cent (52 accused persons) were unemployed, nine of whom did not receive benefits. Accused referred for accommodation were more likely to be current social work clients (61 per cent compared with 31 per cent of all those interviewed by the bail information officer). At the same time a higher proportion of accommodation referrals had no current or previous social work contact (24 per cent compared with nine per cent of all bail interviewees).

After discussion of the case with the bail information officer, the bail accommodation officer recorded problems of relevance to the securing of an accommodation placement. These are summarised in Table 4.1 which shows that almost half of those referred for accommodation were assessed as having no problems which might influence accommodation provision. A number, however, had family problems, such as separation from partners or loss of contact with family members. It was not unusual for those with mental health problems to be alienated from family and to have a range of other problems too.

Table 4.1
Problems among accused referred to the bail accommodation scheme

Problems reported	Number of accused (n=62)	% of accused
None	28	45
Family	11	18
Alcohol	10	16
Health	8	13
Mental health	7	11
Violence	5	8
Drugs	2	3

In 49 cases, data were available regarding the types of offences with which the accused had been charged. These are shown in Table 4.2. Since accused could face multiple charges totals exceed the number of accused.

Table 4.2
Offences with which accused were charged

Offence type	Number of accused (n=49)	% of accused
Public order	23	47
Dishonesty	22	45
Violence	16	33
Criminal justice	9	18
Drugs	5	10
Road traffic	4	8
Other	2	4

Forty one accused (66 per cent of accommodation referrals) were recorded as being of no fixed abode. In 22 cases, the reason for the lack of a fixed address was recorded.

Table 4.3
Reasons for accused being of no fixed abode

	Number of accused (n=22)
No verified address available	8
Hostel dweller	7
Apart from family	5
House repossessed	2
No information	19

As Table 4.3 indicates, the bail information officer had been unable to verify the existence of an address for eight accused. In seven cases the accused was currently a hostel dweller. However a number of hostels restricted the length of time residents were able to live in the hostel and some were unable to return for this reason.

Bail information reports were submitted to the court in 46 cases (74 per cent). In most of the 16 cases in which there was no bail information report the bail information officer had been unable to verify any information. In five of these cases a verifiable address had not been provided by the accused and in two other instances a report was not submitted because an alternative address could not be found.

Accused not referred for accommodation

In ten cases (16 per cent) the bail accommodation officer did not consider it appropriate to make a referral to an accommodation agency: all but one of these ten accused were recorded as being of no fixed abode. The bail accommodation officer's reasons for not referring these accused to an accommodation provider were known in six cases. One accused was suicidal; a second had an unsettled lifestyle; one was already known to SACRO (Lothian) as a 'time-waster'; one accused was said to be extremely violent; and one lived outwith the region (which created financial difficulties). Although the sixth accused was said to have an address to return to, he had been ejected from the family home: no further information about his circumstances was provided.

Approaches to accommodation providers

In the remaining 52 cases (84 per cent), the bail accommodation officer attempted to find accommodation for the accused person. Twenty seven approaches were made to Albrae, seven to Allalon and one to each of the two probation hostels. Five approaches were made to landladies and one to both Albrae and a landlady. In the remaining 11 cases approaches were made to various facilities for homeless persons (such as the People's Palace and the Salvation Army) or to specialist accommodation.

Outcome of accommodation referrals

Table 4.4 shows the outcome of approaches made on behalf of the accused.

Table 4.4
Outcome of approaches to accommodation providers

Outcome of referral	Number of accused (n=49)	% of accused
No offer of accommodation	29	59
Offer made	20	41

In around three-fifths of cases no offer of accommodation was made to the accused. Table 4.5 shows the reasons why these 29 accused were not offered accommodation.

Table 4.5
Reasons why accused were not offered accommodation

Reason for no offer of accommodation	Number of accused (n=29)	% of accused
No vacancies/no reply	18	62
Hostel rules	6	21
Address verified	2	7
Accused known to hostel	1	3
Not enough supervision available	1	3
Accused had no income	1	3

As Table 4.5 indicates, in most cases accommodation was not offered either because vacancies were not available or because the bail accommodation officer had not been able to contact accommodation providers. Albrae generally refused referrals because there were no vacancies, but also refused one accused who had no previous convictions, an accused person who required a higher level of supervision than could be offered by the hostel and an accused already known to them who was not welcome back. In one case Albrae offered a place but the bail information officer was able in the interim to locate another address.

Most of the cases in which accommodation was refused on the grounds of hostel rules related to Allalon, which had a policy of working only with accused persons who had pled guilty. One accused was unable to return to the People's Palace due to restrictions on returning to the hostel within a certain period. Usually accommodation in hostels other than the probation hostels was not available because the bail accommodation officer had been unable to contact staff. One landlady refused to accommodate an accused because he had no source of income.

Accused persons offered accommodation

Twenty accused persons were offered accommodation and six became resident. Table 4.6 shows the accommodation offered and the numbers who actually took up residence.

Table 4.6
Accommodation offered to accused person and taken up

Accommodation	Offered (n=20)	Taken up (n=6)
Albrae	12	3
Landladies	5	2
Allalon	1	1
People's Palace	2	0

As Table 4.6 shows, 12 accused were offered accommodation in Albrae but only a quarter became resident. Two of the five referrals to landladies were taken up by accused. In five of the cases in which the accommodation was taken up by the accused, bail was granted with a special condition of residence at the hostel or landlady's address.

Accused persons who did not take up accommodation

The destinations of those 14 accused who were offered accommodation but who did not turn up are shown in Table 4.7. Four accused were granted bail, but to other addresses. In one of these cases the accused had committed an assault against a partner who lived nearby. He was bailed to his home address with a special condition of bail attached. In another case the accused was bailed to his home address although his parents had indicated to the bail information officer that he would not be welcome home.

Table 4.7
Destination of accused who did not take up residence

Destination	Number of accused (n=14)
Accused bailed to different address	4
Released, not on bail	4
Remanded in custody	3
Alternative address found	1
Place no longer available	1
Not known	1

Bail accommodation in Glasgow

The initial focus of the scheme was on the provision of a credible and comprehensive information service to the courts. Once this had been established one bail officer could focus on the development and operation of accommodation for bailees. In the interim a bail officer would visit SACRO (Strathclyde) on a weekly basis.

Part of the remit of the bail officers in Glasgow was to locate, where appropriate, suitable accommodation for bailees. During the planning stages it was agreed that six beds would be made available for bailees through the Hamish Allan Centre. This district council resource offered free overnight bed and breakfast accommodation to clients (including bailees referred by the scheme) who presented as homeless. The following morning caseworkers interviewed clients with a view to locating alternative accommodation which included council and other hostel provision and, for 16 and 17 year olds, furnished accommodation. There were a number of other hostels for homeless persons available including a DSS hostel with 200 beds at Bishopbriggs and the Great Eastern Hotel in Glasgow.

The bail officers were, in addition, able to refer women bailees to the Dick Stewart probation hostel which was prepared to accept bailees, to provide support and to inform the bail officers in the event of a bailee moving out. The

SACRO hostel in Glasgow was also willing to accept bailees.

Despite the ready availability of emergency accommodation in Glasgow to which the scheme had access, a number of difficulties arose. There was, for instance, some uncertainty over what constituted an acceptable address for the court. Accused referred to the Hamish Allan Centre were usually moved on to other accommodation the following day and the bail scheme was not provided with details of the new address. The clerks and fiscals who attended the monitoring and advisory group were able to offer clarification: unless the accused person's address was of special significance (if, for example, there was concern about a threat to witnesses or if the alleged offence had occurred at or near the accused's usual residence) all that was required was an address of citation and it was the responsibility of the accused to notify the court of a change of address. If the court required an assurance that an accused was actually resident at a given address, caseworkers at the Hamish Allan Centre could provide details of move-on accommodation to the bail officers who were then in a position to notify the court.

Staff at the Dick Stewart hostel also identified a number of problems in dealing with bailees. Firstly there appeared to be an assumption by some social workers and by the courts that accused who were bailed to the hostel could continue to reside there after the bail period had ended. The bail officers accordingly agree to stress the temporary nature of the hostel provision in relevant cases.

Secondly, bailees did not necessarily have a social worker and even those who did could find their case reallocated if they moved across geographical boundaries. Hostel staff consequently found themselves taking on tasks that area team social workers would otherwise have undertaken. To prevent additional burdens being placed upon hostel staff the bail officers agreed, following discussion of the issue at the monitoring and advisory group, to contact the local social work office if support for bailees was required.

Finally, bailees could occupy hostel beds for long periods, reducing the availability of a limited resource for other clients and bailees. As a result of discussion at the monitoring and advisory group the bail officers agreed to indicate on the relevant bail information reports that an early diet would be helpful since a hostel had been offered.

Therefore whilst a number of problems arose, they were addressed and generally resolved through discussion at the monitoring and advisory group. The bail officers reported in interview that there was sufficient emergency accommodation available and effective mechanisms existed for placing bailees. As a consequence, lack of accommodation had proved to be a problem in only one case. This said, the bail officers and members of the advisory group were concerned about the suitability of hostel provision. The standard of accommodation in hostels was described as basic and generally poor. Furthermore, other residents in hostel accommodation often had multiple problems. For accused not accustomed to such conditions, hostel accommodation could be distressing. Alternative types of accommodation were also needed for accused who were required by the court to reside at a particular address as a special condition of bail.

The development of accommodation beyond what was currently available proved to be slow and was a source of frustration for the bail officers. Although bail services were a standing item on the agenda for SACRO (Strathclyde) staff meetings and the bail officers had visited the SACRO offices, little progress was made. The Principal Officer (SACRO) had visited a number of city centre boarding houses and reported that in all cases landladies would require a small retainer to keep beds available for the bail scheme. Since no funds were available to pay retainers, the Social Work Services Group of the Scottish Office was approached to ascertain if monies could be made available for this purpose. By the end of the evaluation this matter was still outstanding. In the interim, however, the bail officers had conducted a survey of the accommodation needs of bailees to obtain information on the level of demand for accommodation and the range of accommodation required.

Over a nine month period the bail scheme in Glasgow had established itself as a useful and credible service. The involvement of all the relevant agencies from the planning stage onwards, the involvement of the Assistant District Officer (Courts) both in planning and in the day to day operation of the scheme and the proactive approach of the bail officers meant that problems were identified quickly and solutions reached through discussion with the agencies concerned. The existence of adequate emergency accommodation provided mainly by the district council to some extent masked the difficulties associated with providing suitable accommodation for bailees and it remains to be seen if this issue can successfully be addressed.

In Glasgow, as in Edinburgh, most accommodation activities centred around finding accommodation for accused with family and friends. During the five month monitoring period a total of 98 accused (23 per cent) were identified as requiring other types of accommodation to be found. Most of these (62 accused or 63 per cent) were recorded as being of no fixed abode. A further 35 accused were normally resident within greater Glasgow and one lived in England.

In 67 cases the bail officers were able to verify that a hostel place was available. Twenty-four of these accused (36 per cent) were granted bail at first appearance and a further nine accused (13 per cent) were bailed at second appearance.

Almost three-fifths of accused who had been of no fixed abode but who were offered a hostel place were granted bail (28 accused). By contrast, only three of the 17 accused who had previously resided in the Glasgow area and who were offered a hostel place as an alternative address were bailed.

Since the bail officers were not informed of whether or not accused persons presented themselves at the Hamish Allan Centre the data on bail accommodation are more limited than in Edinburgh.

Summary

A serious problem arose in locating accommodation, other than in probation hostels, for accused in Edinburgh. There was no existing strategy or general resource either for homeless persons or specifically for offenders. In Glasgow there was a pre-existing emergency accommodation service for homeless people. Without such a facility it was extremely difficulty for the bail officers to obtain accommodation for bailees. Both areas, for a variety of reasons, experienced difficulties in developing accommodation beyond what was currently available.

Sixty-two accused persons were referred to the bail accommodation scheme in Edinburgh, two-thirds of whom were recorded as being of no fixed abode. The bail accommodation officer attempted to locate accommodation for 52 accused and in 20 cases an offer of accommodation was made. Only six accused took up residence. Three of the accused who did not make use of the accommodation offered had been remanded in custody, four had been released without a bail order and four had been bailed to a different address.

In Glasgow, accommodation other than with family or friends was sought for 98 accused, just under two-thirds of whom were recorded as being of no fixed abode. The bail officers were able to locate hostel accommodation for two thirds of those for whom an address was required. Almost three-fifths of accused who had been of no fixed abode but for whom a hostel place had been obtained were granted bail by the court.

5 Impact on the use of bail

Introduction

The Manhattan Bail project was aimed at increasing the use made of bail by the courts by providing them with information relevant to the accused person's community ties (employment, family circumstances and so on). This was found to be successful and a number of subsequent studies conducted in England and Wales have similarly suggested that bail information can impact positively upon the court's willingness to grant bail. Some studies (e.g. Godson and Mitchell, 1992; Lloyd, 1992) have shown that bail information schemes can have an influence at various points in the bail decision-making process, by removing the prosecution's opposition to bail, by increasing the number of bail applications by the defence, and by increasing the court's willingness to grant bail in the face of prosecutors' opposition to the defendant being bailed. Information concerning the community ties of persons appearing in court from police detention is most clearly pertinent to the issue of ensuring that the accused will subsequently appear at court as required. Early research conducted in Scotland, however, suggested that prosecutors were more concerned, when opposing bail in court, with the prevention of re-offending by the accused than with whether or not the accused would appear at court (Melvin and Didcott, 1976). This being so, it might be expected that bail information would have a limited contribution to make to the bail/remand decision. More recent Scottish research, on the other hand, has highlighted the differing cultures which exist in different courts with respect to the willingness of criminal justice agencies to adopt a favourable attitude towards bail (Paterson and Whittaker, 1994). The same research illustrated that criminal justice decision-makers placed varying degrees of emphasis upon the relative significance of a range of factors with respect to the bail/remand decision.

When the bail information experiment was introduced in Scotland an objective of both schemes was to reduce the use of custodial remands by the courts. The provision of positive verified information about community ties would, it was hoped, encourage the courts in some cases to grant bail to

71

accused persons who might otherwise face a remand in custody pending a further appearance, prior to sentence or awaiting trial. Estimating the impact of bail information upon bail decisions is a complex task, not least since factors other than verified information are relevant to the bail/remand decision. Before considering whether and to what extent the information contained in bail information reports may have encouraged a more liberal attitude towards the granting of bail it is necessary to compare the characteristics of accused persons who are remanded in custody and bailed.

The characteristics of bailees and custodial remands

Two primary sources of data were drawn upon to identify the factors which distinguish accused persons who were bailed at first appearance from those who were remanded in custody.

SCRO data

The Scottish Criminal Record Office (SCRO) provided details of previous convictions (in the three years prior to the date of first appearance) and subsequent convictions and charges for 299 accused persons who had been approached by the Edinburgh and Glasgow bail officers for interview between 1 November 1991 and 31 January 1992 and who were known to have been remanded in custody or granted bail. By linking these data to the individual data collected from the bail information schemes it was possible to examine the relationship between the bail/remand outcome and a range of variables.

Table 5.1
Bail/remand outcome and previous convictions

| Outcome | Number of previous convictions | | | |
	0	1-3	4-6	7+
Bailed	59 (79%)	47 (62%)	28 (55%)	38 (39%)
Remanded	16 (21%)	29 (38%)	23 (45%)	59 (61%)
Total	75 (100%)	76 (100%)	51 (100%)	97 (100%)

Overall, a clear relationship was found between the likelihood of being bailed or remanded and the number of previous convictions. As Table 5.1 shows, the higher the number of previous convictions, the greater the likelihood of being remanded in custody at first appearance (χ^2=27.8, 3 d.f., p<.001). Accused persons were, in addition, more likely to have been remanded in custody the higher the number of custodial sentences they had served in the previous three years (Table 5.2: χ^2=40.8, 2 d.f., p<.001).

Table 5.2
Bail/remand outcome and previous custodial sentences

Outcome	Number of previous custodial sentences		
	0	1	2+
Bailed	129 (72%)	17 (46%)	26 (31%)
Remanded	50 (28%)	20 (54%)	57 (69%)
Total	179 (100%)	37 (100%)	83 (100%)

As Table 5.3 indicates, accused who had convictions for bail offences in the previous three years were more likely to have been remanded in custody (χ^2=22.2, 2 d.f., p<.001). The level of custodial remand appeared, however, to be unrelated to the number of convictions for bail offences.

Table 5.3
Bail/remand outcome and previous convictions for bail offences

Outcome	Number of convictions for bail offences		
	0	1-2	3+
Bailed	108 (71%)	27 (47%)	37 (42%)
Remanded	45 (30%)	31 (53%)	51 (58%)
Total	153 (101%)	58 (100%)	88 (100%)

The level of custodial remand was higher both among accused persons who had previously been convicted of failure to appear and among those who had been convicted of further offending whilst on bail. Thus 38 per cent of those with no convictions in the previous three years for failing to appear at court as instructed were remanded in custody compared with 65 per cent of those with one or more such convictions (χ^2=11.4, 1 d.f., p<.001). Similarly, 31 per cent of accused persons who had not previously been convicted of re-offending whilst on bail were remanded in custody in comparison with 56 per cent of those who had been convicted on at least one occasion with this type of bail abuse (χ^2=18.8, 1 d.f., p<.001).

With the exception of previous bail abuse, there was no apparent relationship between the bail/remand outcome and the types of offences for which accused persons had been convicted in the previous three years. Nor, for most categories of offences was there a relationship between the nature of the current offence and level of custodial remand. The one exception was road traffic offences, where accused who had been charged with offences of this nature were more likely to have been remanded in custody than those charged with other categories of crime (75 per cent compared with 40 per cent; χ^2=5.8, 1 d.f., p<.02). However, most accused persons who had been charged with road traffic offences were, in addition, facing charges for other types of offences (14/16) and most of these accused had been additionally charged with having committed the alleged offences whilst on bail (11/14).

Accused persons for whom the bail information officers had been able to provide a verified address were less often remanded in custody than those for whom a suitable address had not been confirmed (35 per cent compared with 61 per cent; χ^2=15.9, 1 d.f., p<.001). A comparison was finally made between the outcomes of cases in which the fiscal was opposed to bail and those in which bail was not opposed (including those with a successful address check by the bail information scheme). Accused persons for whom bail was opposed were more likely than others to have been remanded in custody (48 per cent compared with 12 per cent; χ^2=11.2, 1 d.f., p<.001).

Differences emerged between the two schemes, however, in relation to the types of factors which distinguished accused persons remanded in custody and bailees. In Edinburgh, for example, the level of custodial remand did not differ significantly according to whether or not bail was opposed. It is possible, however, that as in the case of fiscal-requested address checks in Glasgow, fiscal attitudes had altered in some instances following the receipt of verified information.

74

Table 5.4
Factors associated with bail/remand outcome in Glasgow and Edinburgh

	Glasgow	Edinburgh
No. of previous convictions	yes	no
No. of custodial sentences	yes	yes
Convictions for 3(1)(a) offences	yes	no
Convictions for 3(1)(b) offences	yes	no
PF opposition	yes	no
Verified address	yes	no
Current bail offences	yes	no

The main differences between Glasgow and Edinburgh in the factors that appeared relevant to the bail/remand decision are summarised in Table 5.4. The most striking difference between the Glasgow and Edinburgh data is the importance of previous and current abuse of bail to the bail/remand decision in Glasgow and its apparent lack of significance in Edinburgh.

Court monitoring data

To locate the work of the bail information schemes in a wider context and to examine trends in the use of bail and custodial remand prior to and following the introduction of the schemes, details were collected from the court calendars of all custody court cases in Edinburgh and Glasgow Sheriff Courts for two two-week periods before and during the operation of the bail information schemes. The four two-week periods involved were 26.11.90-7.12.90 and 28.1.91-8.2.91 ('before' period) and 25.11.91-8.12.91 and 27.11.92-9.2.92 ('after' period'). The data collected for each case included: date of appearance; date of birth; type of warrant; number of charges; nature of main charge; current breaches of bail; plea; bail/remand outcome; outcome of appearance (continued for further enquiries, trial date set etc.); date of next appearance; and, where relevant, sentence passed.

The overall sample consisted of 2522 cases: 1069 in Edinburgh and 1453 in Glasgow. A total of 183 cases were excluded from further analyses either because the type of warrant was unknown or because they did not fall into the categories of cases that might be targeted by the bail information schemes (this included, for example, invitation warrants and bail applications or reviews).

75

With these cases excluded, the total sample consisted of 1033 summary and petition cases in Edinburgh and 1306 in Glasgow. The broad characteristics of the sample, by court, are summarised in Tables 5.5 and 5.6.

Edinburgh Sheriff Court was characterised by: a higher percentage of females ($\chi^2=7.5$, 1 d.f., p<.01); a higher percentage of summary warrants ($\chi^2=9.2$, 1 d.f., p<.01); a higher average number of charges (t=9.9, p<.01) and a higher incidence of current bail offences $(3(1)(a);\chi^2=8.2$, 1 d.f., p<.01: $3(1)(b)$; $\chi^2=8.0$, 1 d.f., p<.01).

Table 5.5
Characteristics of court monitoring cases

	Edinburgh	Glasgow	Total
Mean age (years)	25	25	25
% under 21 years	36	37	36
% male	94	97	96
% summary warrant	80	74	76
Mean number of charges	3.0	2.8	2.9
% current bail offence (3(1)(a))	8	5	6
% current bail offence (3(1)(b))	29	24	26
% not guilty plea	73	79	76

These differences between the courts are consistent with the different types of cases dealt with by the sheriff courts in Glasgow and Edinburgh. Less serious cases involving petty persistent offenders which are referred to the sheriff court in Edinburgh are likely to be heard by the Stipendiary Magistrate in Glasgow. The main offences with which the accused had been charged are summarised in Table 5.6. The two courts were found to differ according to the nature of the main charges faced by accused ($\chi^2=28.5$, 8 d.f., p<.001). Higher proportions of accused in Glasgow were facing charges involving violence or the misuse of drugs while higher proportions of accused in Edinburgh had been charged with offences against public order.

Table 5.6
Main charges by court (court monitoring)

	Edinburgh	Glasgow	Total
Dishonesty	47%	45%	46%
Violence	20%	22%	21%
Public order	12%	9%	10%
Road traffic	9%	8%	9%
Drugs	4%	9%	7%
Criminal justice	3%	3%	3%
Sexual	1%	1%	1%
Firearms/explosives	<1%	<1%	<1%
Other misc.	4%	2%	3%

The outcomes of court appearances are summarised in Table 5.7, while Table 5.8 shows the percentages of accused in relevant cases who were bailed, remanded in custody and ordained and Table 5.9 summarises the disposals received by accused who pled guilty and were immediately sentenced.

Table 5.7
Outcomes of court appearances (court monitoring)

	Edinburgh	Glasgow	Total
Trial	51%	50%	51%
Cont. further enquiries	18%	25%	22%
Sent. def. (reports)	11%	11%	11%
Sentenced	10%	8%	8%
Sentence deferred	4%	2%	3%
Continued without plea	2%	2%	2%
Fully committed	2%	<1%	1%
Other	2%	2%	2%

The 'other' category in Table 5.7 includes cases in which a guilty plea was accepted, those which were dismissed, deserted or in which no further proceedings were taken, pleas to relevancy or competence, proof hearings and debates. The most noticeable difference between the two courts was in relation to the percentage of cases continued for further enquiries, which reflects the higher percentage of petition cases in Glasgow Sheriff Court.

Table 5.8
Bail/remand outcome by court (court monitoring)

	Edinburgh	Glasgow	Total
Standard bail	56%	59%	58%
Special bail	5%	3%	4%
Remanded in custody	26%	31%	29%
Ordained	13%	7%	10%

The two courts differed in the percentages ordained and remanded in custody (χ^2=37.2, 3 d.f., p<.0001), presumably reflecting the higher proportion of petition cases in Glasgow and, because of the existence of the Stipendiary Magistrate's Court in that city, the generally more serious nature of summary cases appearing before the Sheriff Court. As Table 5.9 shows, accused who pled guilty and were sentenced were more likely to have received a custodial sentence in Glasgow than in Edinburgh (χ^2=17.6, 2 d.f., p<.001).

Table 5.9
Main penalty by court (court monitoring)

	Edinburgh (n=98)	Glasgow (n=97)	Total
Monetary	76%	47%	62%
Custody	14%	37%	26%
Other non-custodial	10%	16%	13%

In total, 1892 cases were bailed or remanded in custody: 785 in Edinburgh and 1107 in Glasgow. As Table 5.10 clearly indicates, in both courts the likelihood of being bailed was higher the lower the number of offences with which the accused had been charged (Edinburgh; χ^2=25.6, 3 d.f., p<.0001:

78

Glasgow; χ^2=18.6, 3 d.f., p<.001).

Table 5.10
Percentage bailed by number of charges (court monitoring)

Number of charges	Edinburgh	Glasgow
1	157 (83%)	251 (75%)
2	148 (72%)	185 (65%)
3-5	202 (66%)	250 (64%)
6 or more	48 (57%)	51 (54%)
Total	555 (71%)	737 (67%)

In both courts, accused were more likely to be bailed if they had been charged with summary offences. In Edinburgh, 77 per cent of summary cases and 53 per cent of petition cases were released on bail (χ^2=42.2, 2 d.f., p<.0001). The comparable figures in Glasgow were 74 per cent and 50 per cent (χ^2=62.0, 2 d.f., p<.0001).

Table 5.11
Percentage bailed and current bail offences (3(1)(b))

Current bail offence (3(1)(b))	Edinburgh	Glasgow
Yes	150 (60%)	145 (54%)
No	405 (76%)	592 (71%)
Total	555 (71%)	737 (67%)

The likelihood of being bailed did not differ according to the age or gender of the accused or the nature of the main charge. Nor were accused who had been charged with failure to appear at court whilst on bail less often bailed than those who faced no such charges. However as Table 5.11 shows, in both

79

courts accused who had been charged with committing their current offences whilst on bail were less likely than other accused to be bailed (in both cases, p<.0001). In Table 5.11 the percentages are based upon 783 cases in Edinburgh and 1106 in Glasgow since in three cases the accused had been charged with a bail offence but the type of offence - 3(1)(a) or (b) - was unknown.

It is also instructive, however, to examine whether different factors were associated with the likelihood of being bailed or remanded according to the form of continuation. For this purpose, three main groups of accused can be identified: those who pled not guilty and were remanded/bailed pending trial (1108 cases); those who made no plea or declaration and were bailed/remanded for further enquiries (509 accused); and those who pled guilty and were bailed/remanded for reports (194 accused).

Table 5.12
Percentage bailed prior to trial by number of charges
(court monitoring)

Number of charges	Edinburgh	Glasgow
1	98 (94%)	176 (86%)
2	116 (85%)	116 (77%)
3-5	141 (73%)	161 (74%)
6 or more	32 (65%)	32 (60%)
Total	387 (80%)	485 (78%)

Several factors were found to be associated with the likelihood of an accused being bailed or remanded prior to trial. In both courts, the lower the number of current charges, the greater the likelihood of bail (Table 5.12 : Edinburgh, χ^2=27.1, 3 d.f., p<.0001; Glasgow, χ^2=19.6, 3 d.f., p<.001).

As Table 5.13 indicates, in both courts, accused who faced charges of re-offending whilst on bail were less often bailed than other accused who tendered not guilty pleas and had trial dates set. (In Edinburgh, χ^2=23.6, 1 d.f., p<.0001; in Glasgow, χ^2=33.0, 1 d.f., p<.0001).

Table 5.13
Percentage bailed prior to trial and current bail offences (3(1)(b))
(court monitoring)

Current bail offence (3(1)(b))	Edinburgh	Glasgow
Yes	106 (68%)	98 (61%)
No	281 (87%)	387 (83%)
Total	387 (80%)	485 (78%)

Accused who faced petition charges and who made no plea or declaration were less likely in both schemes to be bailed if they had been charged with the commission of further offences whilst on bail. In Edinburgh, bail was granted to 59 per cent of accused whose cases were continued for further enquiries and who had not been charged with re-offending whilst on bail and to 25 per cent of accused who had been charged with 3(1)(b) bail offences (χ^2=13.2, 1 d.f., p<.001). The difference was less marked in Glasgow where the comparable figures were 53 per cent and 36 per cent respectively (χ^2=5.3, 1 d.f., p<.05).

In Edinburgh, but not in Glasgow, the likelihood of being granted bail pending further enquiries decreased with the number of current charges (for example, 68 per cent of those facing one charge were bailed compared with only 19 per cent of those facing six or more; χ^2=16.0, 3 d.f., p<.01) and younger accused were more likely than those aged 21 or over to be bailed (χ^2=16.0, 2 d.f., p<.001). In Glasgow, on the other hand, women accused were less often remanded for further enquiries than men (25 per cent compared with 52 per cent; χ^2=4.3, 1 d.f., p<.05).

Overall, 62 per cent of accused who pled guilty and for whom sentence was deferred for reports were bailed (63 per cent in Edinburgh and 61 per cent in Glasgow). Whether accused were bailed or remanded for the preparation of reports did not appear to be related to any of the factors previously discussed.

Bail information and bail decisions

In the present section, data from a range of sources are examined to assess whether the provision of verified information by schemes had led to the release on bail of accused who would otherwise have been remanded in custody.

81

SCRO data

SCRO, as previously noted, provided additional data for a sub-sample of 299 bailees. As in the wider sample of cases included in the monitoring period, accused persons for whom fiscals were at least initially opposed to the granting of bail were more likely, in both schemes, to have been bailed if the bail information officer submitted a report containing only positive verified information (Table 5.14).

Table 5.14
Percentage of cases bailed and nature of bail information
(PF opposed cases)

	Edinburgh	Glasgow	Total
Positive information	71% (47/66)	62% (69/109)	66% (115/175)
Other*	42% (11/26)	21% (10/47)	29% (21/73)
Total	63% (58/92)	50% (78/156)	55% (136/248)

* Includes no report, no information verified, negative information and mixed information

It was previously shown, however, that the likelihood of a custodial remand differed according to certain characteristics of the accused. It is possible, therefore, that the accused for whom positive verified information had been provided differed from other accused in other important respects and that these variations, rather than the bail information report, accounted for differences in the willingness of the courts to grant bail.

In Edinburgh, the only factor found to be reliably related to the bail/remand decision was previous custodial experience. A comparison of custodial experience in the two groups of accused revealed that although fewer accused in the group for whom positive verified information had been provided had served one or more previous custodial sentences (36 per cent compared with 68 per cent) this difference was not statistically reliable (p=0.30). It would appear, therefore, that the differential granting of bail among accused in Edinburgh who had positive information verified by the bail information officer and those who did not cannot be attributed to other relevant differences between the two groups of accused.

In Glasgow, the situation was potentially more complex, since a range of factors appeared to be related to the court's willingness to grant bail. Indeed those accused who had positive information verified were, on the basis of other characteristics, found to have been less at risk of a custodial remand than other accused who were interviewed by the scheme: the former were more often first offenders, had fewer previous convictions, were less likely to have been imprisoned in the previous three years and were less likely to have had previous convictions for bail offences (both 3(1)(a) and (b)). These differences alone might have accounted for the observed difference in the level of bail between the two groups.

To test this possibility further, the bail/outcomes by types of information verified (positive or other) were examined while controlling, in turn, for the effects of these other variables. The results of these analyses are summarised in Tables 5.15 - 5.18.

Table 5.15
Percentage granted bail, bail information and previous convictions (Glasgow)

	Number of previous convictions		
	0	1-6	7+
Positive information	86% (30/35)	56% (24/43)	45% (14/31)
Other	50% (1/2)	32% (7/22)	9% (2/23)

As Table 5.15 shows, accused were more likely to be granted bail if positive information was provided by the schemes regardless of the number of previous convictions. The data for accused persons with no previous convictions are of limited reliability because of the small number concerned (only two accused in the 'other' category had no previous convictions in the three years prior to sentence). Among those with previous convictions, however, accused for whom positive information had been provided were more often bailed than other accused (χ^2=10.2, 1 d.f., p<.01), with this difference being most marked among accused with seven of more convictions in the previous three years (χ^2=6.7, 1 d.f., p<.01). Rather than the number of previous convictions accounting for differences in the granting of bail between the two groups of accused, it appears that the provision of positive verified information resulted in an increased use of bail, especially for those accused with more extensive police records.

In Table 5.16 the relationship between the type of information provided by the schemes and the percentage of accused bailed is examined separately for three groups of accused: those who had served no custodial sentences in the previous three years; those who had served one custodial sentence; and those who had previously been sentenced to periods of imprisonment on two or more occasions. In each group, accused were significantly more likely to have been granted bail if a bail information report containing positive verified information had been submitted to the court (in each case, p<.05).

Table 5.16
Percentage granted bail, bail information and previous custodial sentences (Glasgow)

	Number of previous custodial sentences		
	0	1	2+
Positive information	77% (51/66)	44% (7/16)	37% (10/27)
Other	50% (9/18)	- (0/8)	5% (1/21)

Table 5.17
Percentage granted bail, bail information and previous failure to appear (Glasgow)

	Previous convictions for failure to appear	
	yes	no
Positive information	28% (5/18)	69% (63/91)
Other	18% (3/17)	23% (7/30)

When the accused had no convictions in the previous three years for 3(1)(a) bail offences (failure to appear), bail was more likely to have been granted if positive verified information had been provided by the bail information scheme (Table 5.17; χ^2=17.6, 1 d.f., p<.001). However, the existence of verified information appeared to make little difference to the

84

granting of bail if the accused had been previously been convicted of failing to appear at court when previously subject to a bail order (χ^2=0.1, 1 d.f., p=.75), with the majority of accused being remanded in custody under these circumstances (Table 5.18).

Table 5.18
Percentage granted bail, bail information and previous offending on bail (Glasgow)

	Previous convictions for offending on bail	
	Yes	No
Positive information	45% (21/47)	75% (47/62)
Other	13% (4/30)	35% (6/17)

A different pattern emerges, however, when the granting of bail is examined separately for accused with previous convictions for offending whilst on bail and those with no such previous convictions. Bail was more often granted if positive verified information was provided both in the case of accused with no previous convictions for 3(1)(b) offences (χ^2=8.2, 1 d.f., p<.01) and in the case of those with one or more such convictions in the previous three years (χ^2=6.9, 1 d.f., p<.01).

Taken together then, these findings suggest that in both Glasgow and Edinburgh, accused were more likely to be granted bail if a bail information report containing positive verified information was submitted to the court. In Glasgow, positive verified information appeared unrelated to the granting of bail only for those accused who had previously been convicted of failing to appear at court as required, a finding which is consistent with the greater importance apparently attached to such offences when deciding whether or not to grant bail in Glasgow Sheriff Court.

It is possible, finally, to obtain an approximate estimate of how much of an impact the provision of positive verified information had upon the granting of bail. Across the two schemes, the fiscal's attitude to bail was known in 255 cases (156 in Glasgow and 99 in Edinburgh). As Table 5.14 showed, in cases in which bail was opposed by the fiscal 23 per cent of accused without positive bail reports were granted bail by the courts. If the provision of positive verified information had no effect, then of the 175 accused who had reports containing such information submitted, approximately 50 (29 per cent of 175) could have been expected to have been bailed. In fact, 115 accused were granted bail, suggesting that 64 accused may have been bailed on the strength of positive verified information. In other words it is estimated that 25 per cent (64/255) of interviews by bail officers resulted in the granting of bail to accused who would otherwise have been remanded in custody. When the same reasoning is applied separately to the Edinburgh and Glasgow schemes, then bail information is estimated to have had an impact in 19 per cent and 29 per cent of cases respectively. If address checks are excluded (since many accused in these cases would be bailed following an overnight remand) and similar calculations applied, then bail information is estimated to have had a positive impact in 22 per cent of cases overall and in 23 per cent and 19 per cent of cases in Glasgow and Edinburgh respectively.

Court monitoring data

Details of custody court cases in Edinburgh and Glasgow were collected for two two-week periods before and after the introduction of the bail information schemes. Table 5.19 summarises the court outcomes (bail, remand in custody, ordained) for the two four-week blocks ('before' and 'after') for a total of 2091 accused on summary and petition charges whose outcomes were known. Overall, there appears to have been a slight, but significant, increase in the percentage of offenders bailed (attributable largely to an increase in the use of bail with special conditions) and a decrease in the percentage of offenders ordained to appear for sentence or trial (χ^2=16.9, 3 d.f., p<.001).

Table 5.19
Outcome of appearance by monitoring period (court monitoring)

	Block	
Outcome	Before	After
Standard bail	555 (58%)	657 (58%)
Special bail	21 (2%)	59 (5%)
Remand in custody	280 (29%)	320 (28%)
Ordained	106 (11%)	93 (8%)
Total	962 (100%)	1129 (99%)

86

A different pattern is evident, however, when the before and after data are examined separately by court. As Table 5.20 indicates, there were slight increases in the use of standard bail, special bail and custody during the second monitoring period in Edinburgh and a more substantial decrease in the percentage ordained (χ^2=10.1, 3 d.f., p<.02).

Table 5.20

Outcome of appearance by monitoring period (Edinburgh)

Outcome	Block Before	After
Standard bail	229 (54%)	277 (58%)
Special bail	19 (4%)	30 (6%)
Remand in custody	103 (24%)	127 (26%)
Ordained	70 (17%)	47 (10%)
Total	421 (99%)	481 (100%)

Table 5.21

Outcome of appearance by monitoring period (Glasgow)

Outcome	Block Before	After
Standard bail	326 (60%)	380 (59%)
Special bail	2 (<1%)	29 (4%)
Remand in custody	177 (33%)	193 (30%)
Ordained	36 (7%)	46 (7%)
Total	541 (100%)	648 (100%)

In Glasgow, on the other hand, there was a slight decrease over the twelve month period in the percentages granted standard bail or remanded in custody while the use of bail with special conditions increased and the percentage ordained remained largely unchanged (Table 5.21; χ^2=20.1, 3 d.f., p<.001).

While other factors (such as changes in prosecution policy) may have contributed to the pattern of outcomes across the two monitoring periods it is also possible that some 'net-widening' may have occurred in Edinburgh as a consequence of the introduction scheme. That is, the provision of bail information reports may have resulted in some accused persons who would otherwise have been ordained being granted bail pending their next court appearance. Such net-widening would be less likely in Glasgow where bail information interviews were conducted exclusively with accused for whom the fiscal was at least initially opposed to the granting of bail.

When cases in which the accused was ordained to appear for trial or sentence are excluded, it is clear that there was no significant decrease in the percentages of accused remanded in custody as opposed to being bailed following the introduction of the bail information schemes. In Edinburgh, identical percentages of accused were remanded in custody in the two monitoring periods (29 per cent) and although in Glasgow a slightly lower percentage were remanded in custody after the introduction of the schemes (32 per cent compared with 35 per cent the previous year), this difference was not statistically reliable (χ^2=1.0, 1 d.f., p=.32).

In Edinburgh significantly fewer females were represented in the 'after' monitoring period (4 per cent compared with 7 per cent). However, there was no evidence that in Edinburgh women were significantly less likely than men to be remanded in custody for further enquiries, while awaiting trial or for the preparation of reports. The characteristics of the Edinburgh sample did not otherwise differ across the two monitoring periods in ways which would suggest that the more recent sample were in certain respects more at risk of being remanded in custody.

In Glasgow, however, the 'before' and 'after' samples differed in two interesting respects: the second monitoring period contained a lower proportion of petition cases and a higher proportion of accused who had been charged with further offending whilst on bail. Both these factors were shown to be related to the likelihood of an accused in Glasgow Sheriff Court being remanded in custody or bailed.

The percentages bailed and remanded in custody in Glasgow before and after the introduction of the bail information scheme were, therefore, compared separately for petition and summary cases and for accused with and without current charges of re-offending on bail. None of the four comparisons revealed a significant decrease in the use of custodial remands in the second monitoring period suggesting that the level of custodial remand remained broadly similar over time for warrant cases, for petition cases, for accused with current bail offences (3(1)(b)) and for those without such offences.

Unlike the data provided by SCRO, the court monitoring data do not indicate that higher percentages of accused in Glasgow and Edinburgh had been granted bail as opposed to being remanded in custody. However, bail information reports are submitted to the court in a only relatively small proportion of cases (during the court monitoring period reports were submitted for 13 per cent of accused in Edinburgh and 7 per cent in Glasgow) and in as many as half of these cases, the accused will be remanded in custody. Furthermore, in a proportion of those remaining, bail would have been granted in any case without the additional information contained in the bail information report. If it is assumed, for the sake of argument, that in a particular week 150 accused appeared before the custody court, then 12 accused may have been interviewed by a bail information officer. It was previously estimated that around a quarter of interviews would result in an accused being released on bail rather than being remanded in custody. Three of these 12 accused may, therefore, have been bailed as a result of positive verified information being provided to the court. This accounts, however, for only two per cent (3/150) of all cases appearing before the custody court that week. It is hardly surprising, therefore, that bail information appears to have had a limited impact upon the use of custodial remand when assessed against the total volume of cases being dealt with by the custody courts.

Information from sheriffs

Prior to the start of the evaluation, fiscals in Glasgow and Edinburgh agreed in principle to indicate, for a limited period of time, whether their attitudes towards the granting on bail were altered, in individual cases, by the information provided in bail information reports. With subsequent changes in the point at which bail information became available to fiscals - reports were made available in court rather than prior to the marking of cases - it was clear that in Edinburgh the main impact of bail information upon the bail decision would be at the point at which sentencers, having considered the arguments put forward by the prosecution and defence, reach a decision regarding the granting or otherwise of bail. In Glasgow, bail information might impact either upon the fiscal's attitude towards bail (especially in the case of address checks) or upon the sheriff's decision in cases in which bail is opposed.

In both sheriff courts an exercise aimed at assessing the importance of bail information to the bail decision was implemented for a limited period of time. A brief monitoring form was attached to the bail information report which invited sheriffs to indicate (by a tick) whether, in the absence of the information contained in the bail information report, their decisions regarding the granting or otherwise of bail would have been different. Sheriffs were also able, if they wished, to offer additional comments on the usefulness of the information contained in individual bail information reports.

The exercise was instituted in Edinburgh Sheriff Court between 1st November 1991 and 31st January 1992 and in Glasgow Sheriff Court during the months of January to March 1992 (to make allowance for the later introduction of the bail information service in Glasgow). Participation in the exercise was at the discretion of individual sentencers. Sixteen forms were completed by sheriffs in Glasgow (out of a total of 166 reports submitted during the relevant period). The participation rate of Edinburgh sheriffs was higher but the forms were accidentally disposed of by a court official before being returned to the researchers. To remedy this situation, the Sheriff Clerk invited sheriffs to comment retrospectively (in February 1992) on the usefulness of bail information reports that had been submitted to them during in the three month period during which the exercise had initially taken place. A total of 52 forms (out of a possible total of 180) were completed retrospectively by sheriffs in Edinburgh. The number of completed forms was, therefore low (especially in Glasgow) and the accuracy of those completed in Edinburgh will have been affected to an unknown extent by the retrospective method of data collection. It is with these caveats in mind that the findings must be interpreted.

Table 5.22
Outcome at first appearance

	Glasgow	Edinburgh	Total
Bail	12	22	34
Remand (further enquiries)	-	24	24
Bail refused	2	2	4
Remand in custody pending trial	-	3	3
Ordained	-	1	1
Not known	2	-	2
Total	16	52	68

As Table 5.22 shows, half the completed forms related to accused persons who were granted bail by the courts. The majority of those who were not granted bail were remanded in custody for further enquiries. In four cases the reason for custodial remand (further enquiries or awaiting trial) was unknown and in two cases the bail/remand decision was unavailable.

Table 5.23
Information verified in reports

	Glasgow	Edinburgh	Total
Address	11	45	56
Current drug/alcohol counselling	3	7	10
Previous SW involvement	-	10	10
Current SW involvement	-	9	9
Employment	-	6	6
Current psychiatric treatment	1	1	2
Good family support	-	2	2
Family illness/bereavement	2	-	2
Family problems	1	1	2
Other	-	5	5
None	2	1	3

The types of information verified in this sub-sample of bail information reports are summarised in Table 5.23. Despite the small sample size, these findings are consistent with the earlier observation that a wider range of information was being verified by the Edinburgh scheme. Column totals in Table 5.23 exceed the number of reports in each court since just under half the reports contained more than one item of verified information. The 'other' category includes: suicide risk (one case); children received into care following offence (one case); emotional problems (one case); sole carer of child (one case); and poor response to probation (one case). Three reports contained no verified information.

In just under a quarter of cases (16) sheriffs indicated that their bail/remand decision would have been different in the absence of the information contained in the bail information report. In all but one of these cases the verified information had been instrumental in the granting of bail by the court. In one case the sheriff was unsure whether his/her decision would have been different while in the remaining 51 cases the decision to grant or withhold bail would have been the same regardless of whether or not the verified bail information was available.

Bail was granted in 19 of these 51 cases, one person was ordained to appear

91

for trial and 31 accused persons were remanded in custody. Bail had not been opposed by the Crown in 12 of the 19 cases in which bail was granted. By contrast, fiscals had been opposed to the granting of bail in all but one of the cases in which the accused was remanded in custody.

Table 5.24
Whether sheriffs' decisions would have been different in the absence of verified information (PF opposed bailees only)

	Glasgow	Edinburgh	Total
Yes	5	9	14
No	4	3	7
Total	9	12	21

Most relevant to an assessment of the impact of bail information upon sentencers' decisions are those cases in which bail was opposed by the Crown but subsequently granted by the sheriff. A total of 21 cases across the two courts fell into this category. As Table 5.24 shows, in two thirds of these cases the sheriffs indicated that their decisions would have been different (i.e. the accused would have been remanded in custody) if the verified information contained in the bail information report had not been available.

Although the overall numbers were small, these data suggest that in certain cases the information provided by the bail information officers was instrumental in securing the release on bail of accused persons who would otherwise have been remanded in custody.

The usefulness of the verified information was addressed in the additional comments offered by sheriffs in 19 cases. While one sheriff expressed dissatisfaction with the method of verification that had been employed (a telephone call rather than a personal visit to confirm an address) the majority of comments related to the usefulness of the information contained in the reports. The bail information report was described in six cases as 'helpful' or 'useful' and in two others the information was said to be 'decisive'. In two cases the information that had been verified had helped to clarify the situation and in two others the confirmed availability of an address was said to have been 'influential' in the granting of bail. One sheriff commented that the bail information report had usefully served to confirm statements made by the defence while in another case it was noted that the report had helped the sheriff to reach a 'difficult decision'.

The relevance of the information contained in the report was questioned by sheriffs in four cases. In each of these cases bail was opposed by the Crown and refused on the basis of the accused person's history of offending or previous abuse of bail. As one sheriff commented:

> The report clarified the position relating to accommodation and indirectly the question whether protection of the cohabitee had to be considered closely. However bail was refused on the basis only of alleged contraventions of the Bail Act and his previous record of Bail Act offences. These were not matters to which the report could relate.

Summary

Data provided by the Scottish Criminal Record Office, when combined with information derived from bail worksheets enabled the relationship between various factors and the bail/remand outcome to be explored. In comparison with accused who were remanded in custody, bailees had fewer previous convictions, less prior experience of custody and fewer convictions for bail offences. Accused were more likely to be remanded in custody if bail was opposed by the fiscal and if the bail information officer had been unable to provide the court with a verified address.

The data derived from the custody court calenders in Glasgow and Edinburgh Sheriff Courts over a total of eight weeks enabled the significance of other factors to the bail/remand decision to be explored. Accused were less likely to be bailed the greater the number of current charges faced and accused on summary charges were more often bailed than those on petition. The likelihood of being granted bail was lower among accused who had been charged with committing their current offence/s whilst on bail.

Among the sample of accused for whom the SCRO had provided additional data, interviewees in both schemes for whom bail was at least initially opposed were less likely to have been remanded in custody if a bail information report containing positive verified information had been submitted to the court. This finding could not be accounted for by differences in the characteristics of accused for whom positive verified information had and had not been provided. In Glasgow where, if anything, positive verified information had a greater impact among accused with more extensive criminal histories, such information appeared irrelevant to the bail/remand outcome only if the accused had a history of failing to appear at court: most who did were remanded in custody.

The court monitoring data suggested that there had been a slight increase overall in the use of bail (especially bail with special conditions), a slight decrease in custodial remands and a more noticeable decrease in the percentages ordained to appear for sentence or trial since the introduction of the bail information schemes. In neither Edinburgh nor Glasgow Sheriff Court, however, did there appear to have been a change in the percentages granted bail as opposed to being remanded in custody. However, even if the provision of bail information had had an impact on the relative use of bail and custodial remands it may not have been readily discernible against the total volume of cases dealt with by the custody courts.

Although the numbers were small, feedback from sheriffs in individual cases suggested that the provision of verified information had in several cases been instrumental in the granting of bail. Although the relevance of verified information about accommodation or community ties was questionable if bail was being opposed primarily or solely on the basis of the accused's previous criminal history or previous bail abuse, sheriffs generally expressed favourable comments concerning the usefulness of information contained in bail information reports.

These findings are in line with other studies of the impact of bail information schemes. Godson and Mitchell (1992), for example, found that when bail information reports were provided to the Crown Prosecution Service where the police were opposed to bail, then the CPS were more likely to request bail than when such information was not available (in England, unlike Scotland, the police often indicate their views on bail and the police view is an important factor in determining whether or not the CPS will oppose the granting of bail). Similarly when bail information reports were made available to defence agents there were more applications for bail and these applications were more likely to be successful than when reports were not available. Lloyd (1992) found that the impact of bail information varied between schemes, but that the presence of positive verified information increased both the level of CPS requests for bail, the number of defence applications and the number of cases where bail was granted.

6 Bail abuse

Introduction

There are two main ways in which bail can be abused: by the accused person failing to appear at court or by the commission of further offences whilst on bail. Other conditions of bail may also be breached (through, for example, interference with witnesses) but failure to appear and offending on bail are the primary concerns on those involved in the decision-making process. A number of studies have shown that more accused can be granted bail without an increase in the level of bail abuse. A study of the Manhattan bail project, for example, indicated an increase in the use of bail without an attendant increase in the numbers of accused failing to appear at court (Rankin and Sturz, 1971).

When, in the first major study of bail in Scotland, Melvin and Didcott (1976) advocated the introduction of a more liberal bail policy they did so on the basis that the majority of people deemed to be bad risks for bail did not, in fact, abuse their release on bail, either through re-offending or through failure to appear at court when required. Bail abuse was related to a number of factors such as the number of analogous previous convictions, the employment status of the accused and the absence of a fixed address. Bail abuse was higher where a greater number of charges were involved and where the current charges were for aggravated burglary.

More recently Wozniak et al. (1988) reported an apparent increase in the incidence of recorded bail abuse following the implementation of the Bail (Etc) Scotland Act 1980, though the authors acknowledged that this increase was likely to reflect, to an unknown extent, improvements in police practice in relation to the requirement, when an offender on bail is apprehended for the commission of a further offence, to record in the crime statistics both the new offence and the breach of bail.

Most incidents of bail abuse identified by Wozniak et al. involved re-offending among individuals on bail. In 1986, for example, re-offending whilst on bail accounted for almost 97 per cent of bail offences recorded by the

95

police (Wozniak et al., 1988, p.19). The issue of re-offending by bailees has received particular attention in recent years, with the problem of so-called 'bail bandits' being highlighted by police forces throughout Britain and attendant calls for a tightening up of bail policies. Research in England and Wales suggested that between 10 and 12 per cent of bailees committed offences on bail (Morgan, 1992) and that those most likely to do so were young people facing charges related to car theft or burglary. However even amongst this high risk group, most bailees were not convicted of offending on bail.

If the availability of positive verified information about community ties results in some accused persons who would otherwise be remanded in custody being released on bail, it is important to assess the extent to which these individuals subsequently breach their bail, either through re-offending or through failure to appear, in comparison with other bailees for whom positive verified information has not been provided. In particular, are accused who are released on bail as a result of the additional verified information more at risk than other bailees of breaching the standard conditions of bail?

Method

To enable an assessment to be made of the relative incidence of bail abuse, the Scottish Criminal Record Office (SCRO) provided details of further arrests and convictions among bailees who were targeted by the Edinburgh and Glasgow bail information schemes between 1 November 1991 and 31 January 1992, a three month period during which both schemes were operational and were being monitored as part of the present research. The sample in both schemes included bailees for whom positive information had been verified in addition to those who had refused to be interviewed, those for whom no information could be verified and those for whom the information verified had been negative or mixed.

The lists of bailees were submitted to the SCRO in three monthly batches approximately six months after the date of first appearance to maximise the number of cases that had been disposed of by the time the police computer search was undertaken. For each individual in the sample, SCRO provided, from their computerised records: the dates, nature and outcomes of subsequent convictions, including, where relevant, the offences on which the individual was bailed; the dates and nature of further arrests (pending cases), indicating, where relevant, where a breach of bail had been recorded and the nature of the breach (failure to appear or re-offending); and details of temporary retentions (i.e. all non-disposals and non-recordable convictions which are retained on record for administrative purposes for a maximum of six months).

For each of these cases (and for a sample of accused persons who were interviewed by the schemes but subsequently remanded in custody - see Chapter Five) the SCRO also provided details of convictions and disposals in the three years prior to the date of first appearance to enable a more detailed examination to be made of the factors associated with bail abuse.

To safeguard the anonymity of the data, the SCRO replaced names with bail scheme code numbers and provided details of broad offence categories and disposals rather than specific offences and sentences. Before considering the findings, it is necessary to acknowledge other inherent but important limitations of the data.

First, the data obtained from SCRO relate only to recordable offences. Convictions for less serious (Group VI and VII) offences will not be considered. Second, the SCRO computer lists convictions by date of initial conviction and does not also record the date on which the offence occurred. If a new conviction for a breach of bail is recorded, therefore, it is unclear whether it relates to the period of bail under consideration in the present research or to a previous period of bail.

Third, where bail offences have been listed with pending cases, which are recorded by the date on which the offence was committed or on which the accused was charged, a more accurate estimate can be made of whether the alleged offence occurred prior to or following the date on which the accused was made subject to bail. The level of alleged bail abuse associated with pending cases is, however, likely to be an over-estimate since not all pending cases will result in conviction for the substantive offence and, consequently, for the breach of bail. On the other hand, since only around a third of offences are cleared up by the police (Wozniak et al., 1988) and since further bail offences may have been accumulated by those accused persons whose cases had not been completed when the police search was carried out, the actual level of re-offending on bail is likely to be higher, to an unknown extent, than that indicated by these data.

The SCRO sample

Across the two schemes the SCRO were able to trace the relevant police data for a total of 172 bailees - 79 in Glasgow and 93 in Edinburgh. The characteristics of the sample are summarised briefly in Tables 6.1-3.

Table 6.1
Age and gender of sample

	Edinburgh	Glasgow	Total
Male	89%	96%	92%
Under 21 years	41%	28%	35%
Average age (years)	25.3	27.3	26.2

Table 6.2
Criminal history of sample

	Edinburgh	Glasgow	Total
Average number of previous convictions	4.4	3.1	3.8
No previous convictions	30%	38%	34%
Previous custodial sentence	26%	24%	25%
Previous 3(1)(a)	11%	10%	10%
Previous 3(1)(b)	39%	32%	36%

Table 6.3
Current offences

	Edinburgh	Glasgow	Total
Dishonesty	49%	38%	44%
Crim. justice (inc. bail)	41%	28%	35%
Public order	36%	33%	35%
Violence	32%	33%	32%
Drugs	6%	4%	5%
Road traffic	2%	3%	2%

The column totals in Table 6.3 exceed the number of bailees in each scheme since many bailees had been charged with more than one type of offence. It is clear from comparison with the data presented in Chapter Three that the SCRO samples of bailees were similar in terms of gender and age to the larger samples from which they were drawn. Other data in these tables cannot readily be compared with information presented in earlier chapters since the latter was provided by the accused. However, despite the relatively small sample size there is no reason to suspect that the bail abuse data should be unrepresentative of the larger sample of bailees interviewed by the schemes during the research monitoring period.

The incidence and nature of bail abuse

Overall, 131 of the 172 bailees (76 per cent) had no new convictions recorded for bail offences, while 41 (24 per cent) had one or more convictions for breaches of bail which may or may not have related to the relevant bail period. Similar proportions of bailees in Glasgow and Edinburgh had no new convictions for bail offences (73 per cent of the former and 78 per cent of the latter). The majority of new convictions for bail offences (56/62 or 90 per cent) related to offending while on bail.

A total of 39 bailees (23 per cent) had outstanding charges for breaches of the bail act which they had accrued during their period on bail, most of which (67/69 or 97 per cent) were for further offending. A quarter of the bailees in Edinburgh (25 per cent) and a fifth of those in Glasgow (20 per cent) had been charged with breaching their bail requirements. A further 13 bailees in Edinburgh (14 per cent) and eight in Glasgow (ten per cent) had been charged with further offences whilst on bail but had no additional charges of bail abuse recorded against them. This may reflect delays on the notification to the police of bail being granted by the courts and delays in the updating of bail details by Scottish Police Force Record Offices. It is also important to note that bailees targeted by the schemes were by definition a high risk group and that these figures cannot, therefore, be considered representative of bailees in general.

The types of offences that the 39 bailees were alleged to have committed while on bail are summarised in Table 6.4. Column totals in Table 6.4 exceed the number of bailees since many had been charged with more than one type of offence.

Table 6.4
Types of offences alleged to have been committed by bailees

Offence	Edinburgh (n=23)	Glasgow (n=16)	Total (n=39)
Dishonesty	21	11	32
Public order	12	6	18
Violence	7	1	8
Criminal justice (not bail)	1	2	3
Drugs	1	1	2
Road traffic	-	1	1
Total	42	22	64

Factors associated with alleged bail abuse

By linking the statistical data provided by the SCRO with the information obtained from the bail information worksheets, it was possible to identify which factors were associated with an increased incidence of alleged bail abuse among the sample. The following analyses were based upon a total sample of 156 bailees: 16 bailees who had new convictions which may or may not have related to offences committed during the relevant bail period but who had no other charges that clearly had been accrued while on bail were excluded. The analyses were based, therefore, only upon those bailees were known to have been charged with alleged breaches of bail and those who were known to have had no such charges made against them in the follow-up period.

Age

As Table 6.5 shows, the younger the bailee, the greater the likelihood of having been charged with a breach of bail through the commission of further offences (χ^2=8.7, 2 d.f., p<.02). Just over half of those alleged to have committed a further offence whilst on bail were under 21 years of age.

100

Table 6.5
Alleged bail abuse and age

Alleged bail abuse	Age		
	16-20	21-30	31+
Yes	21 (35%)	13 (22%)	5 (12%)
No	35 (62%)	45 (78%)	37 (88%)
Total	56 (100%)	58 (100%)	42 (100%)

Criminal history

The likelihood of being charged with a breach of bail was also found to be related to a number of factors associated with the previous criminal histories of the bailees. The greater the number of convictions in the three years prior to the date on which bail was granted, the more likely it was that the bailee had been subsequently charged with breaching the conditions of bail (Table 6.6: χ^2=13.1, 3 d.f., p<.01).

Table 6.6
Alleged bail abuse and previous convictions

Alleged bail abuse	Previous convictions			
	0	1-3	4-7	7+
Yes	6 (11%)	10 (23%)	10 (40%)	13 (41%)
No	49 (89%)	34 (77%)	15 (60%)	19 (59%)
Total	55 (100%)	44 (100%)	25 (100%)	32 (100%)

Bailees were, in addition, more likely to have been charged with a breach of bail the higher the number of custodial sentences they had served in the previous three years. As Table 6.7 shows, the incidence of alleged bail abuse was lowest among bailees with no prior custodial experience and highest among those who had previously served two or more sentences of imprisonment or detention (χ^2=7.9, 2 d.f., p<.02).

Table 6.7
Alleged bail abuse and custodial experience

Alleged bail abuse	Number of previous custodial sentences		
	0	1	2+
Yes	24 (20%)	5 (33%)	10 (48%)
No	96 (80%)	10 (67%)	11 (52%)
Total	120 (100%)	15 (100%)	21 (100%)

Bailees who had been convicted in the previous three years of failing to appear at court when requested were slightly, but not significantly, more likely than other bailees to have subsequently been charged with committing offences while on bail (43.8 per cent of the former compared with 22.9 per cent of the latter; χ^2=2.3, 1 d.f., p=.13). Bailees who had previously been convicted of offending whilst on bail were, on the other hand, significantly more likely than those who had no such previous convictions to have been charged with further offences during their present period on bail (40.7 per cent of the former compared with 16.7 per cent of the latter; χ^2=9.7, 1 d.f., p<.01). Moreover, as Table 6.8 shows, the greater the number of previous convictions for bail offences (3(1)(a) and (b)) in the previous three years, the greater the likelihood of a bailee having been charged with an alleged breach during the current bail period (χ^2=10.8, 2 d.f., p<.01).

Table 6.8
Alleged bail abuse and previous breaches of bail

Alleged bail abuse	Number of previous convictions for bail offences		
	0	1-2	3+
Yes	17 (17%)	8 (32%)	14 (45%)
No	83 (83%)	17 (68%)	17 (55%)
Total	100 (100%)	25 (100%)	31 (100%)

Current offence

Table 6.9 summarises the incidence of alleged bail abuse among bailees who had been granted bail while awaiting trial or sentence for different types of offences. Since many offenders had been charged with or convicted of more than one type of offence, the column total in Table 6.9 exceeds the overall sample size of 156.

Table 6.9
Alleged bail abuse and current offence

Current offence	Alleged bail abuse
Criminal justice (inc. bail offences)	20/51 (39%)
Dishonesty	24/65 (37%)
Public order	12/57 (21%)
Violence	11/53 (21%)
Other	2/16 (12%)

Additional analyses confirmed that the incidence of alleged bail abuse was higher among offenders who had been bailed for offences involving dishonesty (χ^2=7.4, 1 d.f., p<.01) or for criminal justice offences (largely bail offences; χ^2=7.1, 1 d.f., p<.01) than among other bailees.

103

Previous offences

The types of previous convictions sustained by those bailees who were not first offenders were found to be related to their likelihood of being subsequently charged with breaches of bail. As Table 6.10 indicates, the incidence of alleged bail abuse was higher the greater the number of convictions for offences involving dishonesty in the previous three years (χ^2=6.3, 2 d.f., p<.05).

Table 6.10
Alleged bail abuse and previous convictions for dishonesty

Alleged bail abuse	Number of previous convictions		
	0	1-3	4+
Yes	4 (18%)	13 (28%)	16 (48%)
No	18 (82%)	33 (72%)	17 (52%)
Total	22 (100%)	46 (100%)	33 (100%)

Supervision as a child

A total of 42 bailees were aged 19 years or less when granted bail. Twelve of this group had been subject to a supervision requirement through the children's hearing system in the previous three years, eight of whom had subsequently been charged with re-offending while on bail. By comparison, just over a quarter of this younger age-group who had had no contact in the previous three years with the children's hearing system (22 bailees) were alleged to have committed further offences whilst on bail (χ^2=4.2, 1 d.f., p<.05).

Factors unrelated to alleged bail abuse

The small number of female bailees in the sample precluded a detailed examination of the relationship between alleged bail abuse and gender. The number of cases (excluding address checks) in which bail was known not to have been opposed by the fiscal was likewise small (six bailees) preventing any firm conclusions from being reached concerning the relationship between fiscal opposition and alleged breach of bail.

The incidence of alleged bail abuse was identical among bailees for whom the bail information officer had been able to verify an address and those whose addresses had not been independently verified by the bail information scheme: 25 per cent of bailees in both groups were subsequently charged with breaches of bail.

Bail abuse: a typology of risk

Several of the factors found to be associated with an increased likelihood of alleged bail abuse - previous convictions, previous custodial experience, previous breaches of bail and number of previous offences involving dishonesty - were found to be highly correlated. A series of discriminant function analyses (which test the predictive ability of a group of variables on the dependent variable - in this case alleged bail abuse) revealed that age, number of previous convictions for dishonesty and number of previous bail offences were together best able to predict whether or not an accused would subsequently be charged with further offending whilst on bail. These three variables correctly classified 74 per cent of bailees.

A further series of analyses used these factors as a basis for classifying the sample according to their risk of alleged bail abuse. Bailees who were aged 25 years or older and who had no convictions in the previous three years were found to present a *low* risk of bail abuse while offenders under 25 years of age with four or more convictions for offences involving dishonesty and/or two or more convictions for bail offences had the *highest* risk of being charged with committing further offences while on bail. The risk of alleged bail abuse was *intermediate* for other groups of bailees.

The relationship between the risk categories and the likelihood of a bailee being charged with further offending on bail is illustrated in Table 6.11 (χ^2=19.6, 2 d.f., p<.001). When this method of classification was applied to the sample as a whole (that is, including both bailees and custodial remands) it was found that almost half the accused who had been remanded in custody (47 per cent) had a high risk of bail abuse compared with just under a quarter of the bailees (23 per cent). Conversely, only eight per cent of those remanded in custody could be classified as having a low risk of breaching bail compared with around a fifth (20 per cent) of bailees. The classification system is necessarily limited by the relatively small sample size upon which it is based. If it assumed, however, that similar proportions of low, intermediate and high risk accused who were remanded in custody on first appearance would have been charged with a further offence had they been bailed, then it is estimated that 34 per cent of custodial remands would have been charged with alleged breaches if they had been granted bail.

Table 6.11
Risk category and alleged bail abuse

Alleged bail abuse	Risk category		
	Low	Intermediate	High
Yes	1 (3%)	21 (23%)	17 (50%)
No	31 (97%)	69 (77%)	17 (50%)
Total	32 (100%)	90 (100%)	34 (100%)

Bail information and bail abuse

A number of factors were clearly identified which were related to the likelihood of bailees being charged with failing to adhere to the conditions of bail. There was no indication, however, that accused persons who were granted bail following the provision of positive verified information were more likely than other bailees to have been subsequently charged with bail offences.

A comparison was made of the incidence of alleged bail abuse among two groups of bailees. The first comprised of those for whom bail had not been opposed and those who had no bail information report submitted or whose bail information reports contained no verified information, negative information or mixed (positive and negative) information. The granting of bail in these cases could not have been affected by the availability of positive verified information in a bail information report. The second group of bailees were those for whom the fiscal was initially opposed to the granting of bail (including address checks) and for whom a bail information report containing exclusively positive information had been provided. In these cases the positive verified information may have been decisive in the sheriff's whether or not to release the accused person on bail.

106

Table 6.12
Alleged bail abuse and bail information

Bail information

Alleged bail abuse	Positive information (PF opposed)	No/negative information or PF not opposed
Yes	26 (25%)	8 (24%)
No	78 (75%)	26 (76%)
Total	104 (100%)	34 (100%)

As Table 6.12 shows, the incidence of alleged bail abuse was almost identical among these two groups of bailees (χ^2=0.0, 1 d.f., p=1.0), suggesting that accused persons who were granted bail and for whom positive verified information had been provided were no more likely subsequently to breach the conditions of bail. There were, in addition, no significant differences between the two groups of bailees when the data were analysed separately by scheme.

It is possible, of course, that the two groups of bailees differed in important respects so that, for example, similar levels of alleged bail abuse were found even though one group was 'riskier' than the other. To exclude this possibility, the two groups were compared with respect to each of the factors previously shown to be related to the likelihood of bailees being charged with bail offences (previous convictions, age etc.). None of these comparisons revealed reliable differences between the groups, suggesting that the two groups were equally risky with regard to the likely incidence of alleged bail abuse. This was confirmed by the finding that similar proportions of bailees in the two groups could be classified as having a low, intermediate or high risk of being charged with bail offences (χ^2=0.5, 2 d.f., p=.77).

Summary

Owing to the manner in which bail offences are recorded in police statistics, it was not possible to obtain an accurate estimate of the incidence of bail abuse among the two samples of bailees. A range of factors were, however, found to be associated with an increased likelihood of *alleged* bail abuse. The likelihood of being charged with bail offences decreased linearly with age and

107

increased with the number of previous convictions, with previous custodial experience and with the number of previous convictions for bail offences. Bailees who had been charged with offences involving dishonesty or with offences against criminal justice (primarily breaches of bail) were more likely than those facing trial or sentence for other types of offences to be charged with further offending while on bail. The higher the number of previous offences involving dishonesty the greater the likelihood of being charged with a breach of bail. With younger bailees (that is those aged 19 years of less) the incidence of alleged bail abuse was higher among those who had been subject to supervision through the children's hearing system in the previous three years.

The factors best able to predict whether or not an accused would be charged with a bail offence were age, the number of previous bail offences and the number of previous convictions for offences involving dishonesty. Accused aged 25 years or over who had no convictions in the previous three years presented the lowest risk of being charged with further offending whilst on bail, while offenders under 25 years of age with several previous convictions for bail abuse and/or offences involving dishonesty presented the highest risk.

There was no evidence, however, that the incidence of alleged bail abuse was higher among accused persons for whom positive information had been verified and who were granted bail despite initial fiscal opposition than among those who were granted bail and for whom positive information about community ties was absent or irrelevant.

These findings are in line with those of other studies though the level of alleged offending on bail in this study is somewhat higher than in previous research (e.g. Morgan, 1992). This might partly reflect different methods of police recording of offending on bail: in Scotland, unlike England and Wales, breach of bail has been an offence since the introduction of the 1980 Bail (Etc) Scotland Act. It was also to be expected, however, that higher levels of apparent bail abuse would have been found in the present study since the cases considered here were, in general, at a higher risk than general populations of bailees.

The factors most closely associated with a higher risk of offending on bail also replicate earlier findings (e.g. Morgan, 1992). However more research is required to untangle further the factors involved in breach of bail: whilst half of those deemed to present the highest risk were charged with breaching bail, half equally were not. To draw upon a typology such as the one outlined in the present chapter in assessing bail risk would result in the courts remanding in custody significant numbers of accused who would not, if they were granted bail, abuse their release.

7 Bail information and final outcomes

Introduction

One argument put forward in favour of reducing the number of custodial remands is that a custodial remand is more likely to lead to a custodial sentence. For example, prison statistics have revealed that most accused who had been remanded in custody did not eventually receive a custodial sentence. Moreover, this was especially true in respect of young people and women (Wozniak et al., 1988). Melvin and Didcott (1976) found that offenders who were remanded in custody prior to trial or sentence were more likely subsequently to receive a custodial sentence than those who were bailed. However, the research subsequently undertaken by Wozniak et al. (1988) reported that only 61 per cent of persons remanded in custody subsequently received a custodial sentence and they pointed to a more complicated relationship between custodial remand and final court outcome, with young offenders who were remanded in custody being less likely than older offenders subsequently to receive a custodial sentence.

The SCRO data

Data provided by the Scottish Criminal Record Office (SCRO) for a sample of 299 accused persons who were targeted by the Edinburgh and Glasgow schemes between 1 November 1991 and 31 January 1992 enabled a comparison to be made of the final court outcomes for bailees and custodial remands and a range of other factors associated with the type of sentence imposed (custodial versus non-custodial) to be identified.

The total sample consisted of 172 bailees and 127 accused persons who were remanded in custody at first appearance (an unknown proportion of the latter group may subsequently have been released prior to trial or sentence). The final outcomes were available for 198 individuals (93 bailees and 105

109

custodial remands, reflecting the shorter average time to trial of the latter).

In 42 cases (23 bailees and 19 remands) no sentence was ultimately passed, usually because the accused had been found not guilty, a not guilty plea had been accepted or the fiscal had decided not to proceed to trial. Just over two-fifths of those who were sentenced (65 individuals or 42 per cent) were given a sentence of imprisonment or detention. As Table 7.1 shows, accused persons who were remanded in custody at first appearance were more likely than those who were granted bail to receive a custodial sentence (χ^2=12.1, 1 d.f., p<.001).

Table 7.1
Final disposal and outcome at first appearance

	Outcome at first appearance	
Sentence	Bailed	Remanded
Custodial	18 (26%)	47 (55%)
Non-custodial	52 (74%)	39 (45%)
Total	70 (100%)	86 (100%)

Factors related to type of sentence

It has previously been shown that accused who are granted bail differ in several notable respects from those who are remanded in custody: the latter, for example, tend to have more extensive criminal histories and to be facing more serious charges. Several factors were likewise found to be related to the type of sentence imposed.

Previous convictions

As Table 7.2 indicates, the likelihood of receiving a custodial sentence was higher the greater the number of convictions in the three years prior to the date of first appearance on the current charges (χ^2=14.6, 3 d.f., p<.01).

Table 7.2
Final disposal and number of previous convictions

Number of previous convictions

Sentence	0	1-3	4-6	7+
Custodial	5 (16%)	12 (35%)	14 (45%)	34 (57%)
Non-custodial	26 (84%)	22 (65%)	17 (55%)	26 (43%)
Total	31 (100.0%)	34 (100.0%)	31 (100%)	60 (100%)

Custodial experience

Accused who had served one or more previous custodial sentence were more likely than those who had no custodial experience to have been sentenced to imprisonment or detention (Table 7.3: χ^2=33.4, 2 d.f., p<.0001).

Table 7.3
Final disposal and previous custodial sentences

Number of previous custodial sentences

Sentence	0	1	2+
Custodial	16 (20%)	13 (62%)	36 (67%)
Non-custodial	65 (80%)	8 (38%)	18 (33%)
Total	81 (100%)	21 (100%)	54 (100%)

Previous bail abuse

Accused who had three or more convictions in the previous three years for bail

111

offences were more likely to receive a prison sentence than those who had fewer than three such convictions or who had no previous convictions for breach of bail (Table 7.4: χ^2=7.0, 2 d.f., p<.05).

Table 7.4
Final disposal and previous convictions for bail offences

Sentence	Number of previous convictions		
	0	1-2	3+
Custodial	20 (32%)	15 (38%)	30 (56%)
Non-custodial	43 (68%)	24 (62%)	24 (44%)
Total	63 (100%)	39 (100%)	54 (100%)

Current offence

As Table 7.5 indicates, the likelihood of imprisonment was generally unrelated to the broad category of offence for which an individual was sentenced. However, offenders sentenced for public order offences were less likely than those convicted of other types of offences to receive a custodial sentence.

Table 7.5
Custodial sentences and current offence

Offence	Custodial sentence	
	Number of offenders	% of offenders
Dishonesty	36/80	45
Violence	20/44	46
Crim. justice (inc. bail)	31/68	46
Public order	13/52	25
Other	7/16	44

Previous offences

For the most part, the likelihood of attracting a custodial sentence was unrelated to the types of previous convictions an offender had. Those who had previous convictions for offences involving dishonesty tended to be more often imprisoned than other offenders (52 per cent compared with 27 per cent) but this difference just failed to achieve conventional levels of significance (χ^2=3.6, 1 d.f., p=.06).

Age

Although young offenders (that is, those aged 16-20 years) were as likely as older offenders to have been remanded in custody at first appearance (see Chapter Five), young offenders were, as Table 7.6 indicates, less likely than those aged 21 years or older to receive a custodial sentence (χ^2=3.9, 1 d.f., p<.05).

Table 7.6
Final disposal and age

	Age (in years)	
Sentence	16-20	21+
Custodial	17 (30%)	48 (48%)
Non-custodial	39 (70%)	52 (52%)
Total	56 (100.00%)	100 (100%)

The age difference in final outcome was, however, restricted to those accused who had been remanded in custody at first appearance. While similar proportions of younger and older bailees were sentenced to imprisonment or detention (23 per cent compared with 27 per cent; χ^2=0.01, 1 d.f.. p=.92) younger offenders who had been remanded in custody were less likely than those aged 21 year or older to receive a custodial sentence (37 per cent compared with 64 per cent; χ^2=4.9, 1 d.f., p<.05).

Final outcome and bail information

It has already been shown that offenders who were remanded in custody at first appearance were more likely subsequently to receive custodial sentences. In not all cases where bail was granted, however, was bail opposed by the fiscal in court. In a few cases in Edinburgh the prosecution had a favourable attitude towards the granting of bail from the outset and in several cases in Glasgow where the lack of a suitable confirmed address was the primary or sole reason for opposition and an address check had been requested, bail was not subsequently opposed by fiscals if the bail information officers were able to verify the accused person's address.

Even when these cases are excluded - that is the sentencing of bailees and remands is compared only for cases involving fiscal opposition for reasons other than a straightforward address check - bailees are still found to have a lower likelihood of attracting a custodial sentence than accused persons who were remanded in custody at first appearance (20 per cent compared with 58 per cent). There was no evidence from the available data, however, that offenders were more at risk of receiving a custodial sentence as a result of their remand status: those who were remanded in custody were found to have more previous convictions (just under a tenth had no previous convictions compared with just under a third of the bailees and just over a half had seven or more previous convictions compared with just under a third of bailees; $\chi^2=10.5$, 3 d.f., p<.02); more custodial experience (just over half had served two or more prison sentences while three-quarters of the bailees had no previous custodial sentences; $\chi^2=25.4$, 2 d.f., p<.001); and more previous bail offences (slightly less than half had three or more convictions for bail offences while just over half the bailees had no previous convictions for breaches of bail; $\chi^2=9.2$, 2.d.f., p=.01). These factors were in themselves related to the likelihood of attracting a custodial sentence. Thus while the provision of verified information to the courts may in some cases have resulted in the granting of bail to offenders who would otherwise have been remanded in custody, it was impossible to conclude whether for these offenders the risk of ultimately receiving a sentence of imprisonment was concomitantly reduced.

Summary

From the data provided by the Scottish Criminal Record Office it was possible to identify the final disposals received by a total of 198 accused. In 42 cases no sentence was passed while just over two-fifths of those convicted received sentences of detention or imprisonment. Accused who had been remanded in

114

custody at first appearance were more likely to subsequently be given a custodial sentence than those who had initially been granted bail. The likelihood of a custodial sentence was greater the higher the number of convictions, custodial sentences and breaches of bail in the previous three years. Offenders who were sentenced for public order offences were less often imprisoned than those sentenced for other categories of offences and those with a history of offences involving dishonesty were slightly, though not significantly, more likely than other offenders to receive a custodial sentence. Finally, young offenders who were remanded in custody were less likely than older offenders (that is, those aged 21 years or over) to attract a custodial sentence. There was no relationship between age and final outcome among accused who had been bailed.

When the final outcomes were compared only for those cases involving fiscal opposition for reasons other than an address check, accused persons who were remanded in custody at first appearance were more often given a subsequent custodial sentence than individuals who were bailed. However, the remands and bailees also differed in such ways as to suggest that the former were, in any case, more at risk of attracting a sentence of imprisonment. It was not possible to determine from the available data whether accused who were bailed on the basis of the information contained in their bail information reports were imprisoned at a lower rate than would have been the case had they been remanded in custody at first appearance. It is possible that fundamental differences between the characteristics of those remanded and those granted bail explain the findings of others (such as Melvin and Didcott, 1976) that accused remanded in custody are more likely to receive a custodial sentence.

From the research outlined in the introduction and the findings described here it seems that the relationship between remand status and final outcome is more complex than would first appear to be the case. More detailed research into this relationship could shed light on the factors which link custodial remands and custodial sentences.

115

8 Perspectives on bail services

Introduction

Previous research studies have highlighted the role that different groups play in the bail process. The prosecutor, whether the fiscal, police or CPS, plays a crucial role in determining which accused are bailed and which remanded; the case put forward in favour of bail by defence agents can influence the judge who in turn makes the final bail/remand decision. How these group view the potential and actual role of bail information and their views on the credibility of such a service are therefore of some significance when attempts are made to evaluate the impact of bail services.

It was anticipated that the introduction of bail services would have an impact upon various agencies closely connected with the bail process. Interviews were conducted with procurators fiscal, with sheriffs and with defence agents since these were the groups most closely involved with the bail information and accommodation experiment. The present chapter summarises their views.

Fiscals' views of bail services

Fiscal members of the two advisory groups were interviewed on two occasions. Initial interviews were conducted shortly after the introduction of the schemes. Subsequent interviews took place one year later in Edinburgh and six months later in Glasgow. At that time interviews were also conducted with two samples of depute fiscals involved in marking custody cases - four each in Edinburgh and Glasgow.

Other than through the attendance of the Assistant Procurator Fiscal at the advisory group, the Edinburgh fiscals' involvement with the scheme was largely confined to the provision to the bail information officer of the names of those whose bail was to be opposed. Fiscals reported having little contact with the bail officer in or out of court.

Most of those interviewed felt that the bail scheme had made little impact on the work of the courts and believed that there was little scope for it to do so. The main value of the scheme lay in locating addresses for accused of no fixed abode or those requiring an alternative address. In cases involving domestic violence in particular it was useful to have independent verification of an address since a victim of domestic assault might agree in court to the accused returning home through fear.

Some fiscals had anticipated that the bail officers would provide a measure of supervision by informing the court if the accused ceased to live at a specific address and were disappointed this had not happened.

The effectiveness the bail information officer's targeting of interviews was questioned by some fiscals. Bail information reports were said on occasion to be unavailable in cases in which bail was opposed and available when bail was not opposed. Concern was expressed that some interviews were conducted with accused who were highly unlikely to be granted bail while in other cases in which verified information could be useful, reports were not available. It was suggested that targeting could be improved if fiscals were able to refer specific cases to the scheme rather than simply providing the names of accused for whom bail would be opposed.

A number of practical problems were highlighted by fiscals. The bail information officer approached them for names at a time when they were particularly busy. Reports had sometimes arrived at the court after the case had been dealt with or were not circulated by the clerk. There were still occasions when cases were continued overnight for information to be checked. Despite these problems it was acknowledged that there had been instances in which bail information reports had been useful and fiscals
thought there might be some value in having verified information available in petition cases at the full committal stage (that is, after a 7 day remand in custody following the initial appearance). There was also considered to be some potential for providing verified information after an accused had pled guilty and bail was being considered for reports. Whilst the fiscal was not technically involved once an accused had pled guilty, she or he could, as an officer of the court, be asked for information by the sheriff. Fiscals also stressed the need for resources to deal with accused persons with mental health

117

problems for whom some form of psychiatric intervention might be of value.

Fiscals did not regard other potential developments as likely to be beneficial. The district court, for example, had fewer bail opposed cases and if bail was opposed the accused would often plead guilty in the expectation that any resulting custodial sentence would be shorter than a custodial remand. Bail hostels or other forms of supervised accommodation would not be particularly useful unless they could match the security of prison conditions. Since bail was only opposed in a small proportion of cases there was little scope for offering less intensive provision in the community: where some measure of supervision was required, this could be achieved satisfactorily through the imposition of bail conditions which could then be enforced by the police.

Glasgow fiscals

Of most value to Glasgow fiscals was the verification by the bail officers of an accused person's address. The bail scheme was considered particularly helpful in finding alternative accommodation for accused, with officers often approaching several potential sources in pursuit of an acceptable address. Verification of an address was of particular importance in petition cases. Prior to the existence of the scheme fiscals would, if doubts existed about an accused person's address at second appearance, request that the case be continued without plea for information to be checked by the police and this usually necessitated an overnight remand. It was pointed out that even if the bail officers were unable to locate an address and the accused was subsequently remanded in custody, the accused was at least aware that strenuous efforts to avoid a custodial remand had been made.

If bail was being opposed on the basis of the individual's record, fiscals were less likely to be influenced by verified information. There were, however, a few cases where evidence of the accused person's trustworthiness (as evidenced, for example, by satisfactory performance of a community service order) could enable the fiscal to adopt a favourable attitude towards the granting of bail. Whilst information of this nature could be provided by the defence, it was unusual for agents to have time to obtain independent verification.

Fiscals contacted the bail officers by telephone at the marking stage as cases in which bail would be opposed were identified. Fiscals reported that, despite initial difficulties in amending their practice, this procedure had now become routine as a result of experience of the bail scheme and regular contact with the bail officers.

The bail officers were regarded as helpful, efficient and 'a pleasure to deal with'. Fiscals appreciated being kept informed of delays in the preparation or non-submission of reports. The reports themselves were described as being clear, concise and containing useful information. The bail officers appeared familiar with the standards of verification required by the court and cited sources and procedures clearly. There was an expectation that bail officers would include negative information where appropriate (though this was not in accordance with the policy of the scheme).

Fiscals were of the opinion that the bail scheme made a valuable contribution to the public interest and to justice. The provision of verified information by the scheme reduced the need to remand accused overnight with savings in the associated costs of prison accommodation, travel and court time. In addition, it was thought that the scheme would reduce the likelihood that an accused would fail to appear by ensuring that an acceptable address was available.

Fiscals were likewise enthusiastic about the possibilities for extending the scheme, particularly to the district court. It was estimated that in the district court two or three cases a day were remanded in custody overnight for addresses to be checked. Custodial remands in such instances were regarded as particularly unnecessary given the more trivial nature of the offences involved. Fiscals were aware there was a social work presence in the district court but this was limited mainly to finding hostel accommodation for young homeless persons: more resources to meet a wider range of accommodation needs would be required.

It was also suggested that defence agents might be permitted to make referrals to the scheme, possibly to request verified information in connection with an accused person's failure to appear. Whilst fiscals would generally accept agents' explanations of why an accused had failed to appear once, following several instances of non-appearance additional verification of the reasons would be required.

Finally, it was thought by fiscals that there could be some value in having verified information available following conviction, both to aid decisions regarding the granting of bail for reports and for sentencing purposes. Whilst not officially involved at this stage of the proceedings, the fiscal might be asked to provide information by the sheriff and was duty bound to correct any gross inaccuracies on the part of the defence.

Sheriffs' views of bail services

In Edinburgh and Glasgow, interviews were conducted with a sample of five sheriffs, including two who were members of the bail scheme advisory groups.

119

Edinburgh sheriffs had very mixed views about the concept and operation of the bail scheme. Most reported they knew little about the aims and operation of the scheme since it had not been fully integrated into the workings of the court. Furthermore they had had little direct contact with the bail officers and little experience of reports. Bail information reports were said to be available only spasmodically, often when bail was not at issue and not when bail was opposed. Various explanations were offered by sheriffs, including inappropriate targeting of reports and the failure of sheriff clerks to provide reports when they were available. Several sheriffs expressed their doubts that there was sufficient work to justify the employment of two full-time staff.

Sheriffs differed in their opinions of the usefulness of bail information. Several pointed out that, even if reports did not lead to the accused being granted bail, having available a source of independently verified information was valuable in helping them reach a decision. At this stage in a case the court generally lacked reliable information about the accused and much decision-making had to be conducted on the basis of assessing probabilities: any scheme such as this which enhanced decision-making was to be applauded. While some sheriffs found the bail information reports they had received to be very useful, well written, concise and focused, others felt unable to comment on the usefulness of the scheme as they had not received reports in cases where bail was at issue.

Sheriffs offered suggestions as to how the scheme might be improved. Better targeting would be welcomed: the scheme, it was suggested, could usefully target cases where an alternative address was required, especially those involving domestic violence. There were, however, mixed views about the need for supervised accommodation or bail supervision, though sheriffs generally agreed there were a small number of young people who could benefit from a more structured environment whilst on bail. The potential value of such supervision had, however, to be balanced against the need to avoid bail being used as a punishment. Moreover, many accused currently remanded in custody would require supervision levels as rigorous as those provided by imprisonment. Despite the difficulty of finding accommodation for bailees in Edinburgh, which sheriffs acknowledged, there was disappointment that there did not appear to be much bail accommodation available.

A final suggestion from the sheriffs was that the scheme should attempt to increase its visibility, preferably by having a bail officer available in court. This would not only increase the credibility and facilitate the integration of the scheme, but would also allow sheriffs to make referrals directly where this was appropriate.

Glasgow sheriffs likewise pointed out that, because they only received bail information reports if bail was opposed, they had relatively little contact with the bail information scheme. The bail scheme was thought to have its impact mainly at the point at which fiscals were forming an attitude towards bail by providing information which overcame fiscals' opposition.

The sheriffs were nevertheless highly appreciative of the bail scheme and some believed that since its introduction there had been reductions both in the proportions of cases in which bail was opposed and in the numbers of cases which were remanded overnight without plea for information (such as addresses offered by the defence) to be checked. Some of the sheriffs had made referrals to the scheme themselves and had found this a useful facility. Defence agents rarely had time to verify information on behalf of clients and some sheriffs expressed reservations about accepting unverified information, whatever the source, in court. Even though prior to the introduction of the scheme court-based social work staff would occasionally supply verified information and locate addresses for accused, this usually necessitated an overnight remand. The existence of the bail scheme meant that information was verified in more cases, providing an independent source of information which helped the court reach better and more reliable decisions about the granting of bail.

Locating accommodation for potential bailees and checking addresses provided by accused was seen as the main function and benefit of the bail scheme. Cases involving domestic and family violence aroused particular concern. Although accused in these cases were often facing minor charges (such as breaches of the peace) and often had no previous convictions, they could not be bailed to the home address. If, however, the bail officers could confirm the availability of alternative accommodation a remand in custody could be avoided. A special condition stipulating that the accused does not approach the victim/s would be included in the bail order to provide the necessary protection required.

Sheriffs varied in the importance they attached to the other types of information which the bail scheme provided. Verification that the accused was seeking help with a drug or alcohol problem could increase the chances of bail being granted. In other instances information about family commitments or bereavements or an update on progress made on community service or probation orders could enhance the accused person's chances of being granted bail.

All the sheriffs spoke very positively about the bail officers whom they described as helpful, flexible, courteous and efficient. One sheriff commented that the bail officers had been realistic in terms of the cases they worked with and attributed the credibility of the scheme at least partly to the fact that they had not sought involvement in cases in which a remand in custody was almost inevitable. In general information was provided quickly and sources and methods of verification were clearly outlined. This helped the court reach a quick and reliable decision about bail.

Sheriffs suggested that bail information might also be helpful when bail was being considered following conviction. Bail information could be particularly useful in the case of accused who were appearing from custody and whose circumstances might have changed as a consequence of the custodial remand.

Views were mixed as to the value of bail hostels and bail supervision. There was some limited support for hostels which might, it was thought, be useful for young people with unstable addresses who could benefit from steady accommodation and some supervision or support. Sheriffs did not believe, however, that the development of such resources would have much impact upon the level of custodial remands.

Finally, there remained two groups for whom provision was limited but for whom additional resources were required: drug users and people with mental health problems. The latter, in particular, presented problems since, in the absence of appropriate accommodation (hospital or other), the fiscal was obliged to remand the accused person in custody for any necessary reports to be prepared.

Defence agents' views of bail services

Interviews were conducted with a sample of defence agents in Edinburgh and Glasgow. Agents on the advisory group in Edinburgh were interviewed on two occasions, once shortly after the introduction of the scheme and again approximately one year later. In Glasgow it was only possible to interview the defence agent on the monitoring and advisory group on one occasion, shortly after the scheme became operational. Interviews were conducted with eight other agents who had had contact with the scheme (four each in Edinburgh and Glasgow). These interviews were held towards the end of the fieldwork period.

Edinburgh defence agents

The defence agents in Edinburgh had mixed opinions of the scheme. Those who found it useful said that verified information and the provision of accommodation had led to some clients being granted bail by the sheriff despite fiscal opposition. Although fiscals varied in their willingness to change their attitude towards the granting of bail there had been instances, even in petition cases, where fiscals had dropped their opposition to bail on receiving verified information. There had also been occasions on which sheriffs had requested bail reports and appeared to have granted bail on the basis of the information contained therein. Where positive verified information concerning progress on community service or probation was available, it provided a challenge to the assumption that the accused was untrustworthy and reinforced the presumption of innocence.

In some cases defence agents had found reports useful at second appearances. For example, bail officers were able to contact hospitals about an accused person's medical condition and appointments and provide a written report. Defence agents often faced delays in getting responses to such requests and, unlike the bail information officer, did not provide the court with the security of an independent written report.

One agent commented that since the introduction of the scheme fiscals paid more attention to the accused person's address. This in itself was thought likely to reduce the likelihood of subsequent failure to appear and made it easier for him to keep in contact with his clients.

Most agents commented, however, that they had little contact with the scheme and were unclear as to how cases were targeted. Reports were often not available when bail was opposed or were late (particularly if cases were dealt with before 12 noon). The absence of a clear pattern to the production of reports was attributed to a lack of resources. Some agents suggested that if they knew that a report was being produced they could request that a case be delayed until it arrived but others were concerned this would slow down the business of the court.

Even if reports were available they were not necessarily distributed in court. One agent reported that he had seen bail information reports on the table, but they had not been handed out. The scheme generally had a low visibility in court and this was said to have damaged its credibility and effectiveness. Occasionally reports were submitted even though no information had been verified and some agents regarded this as a waste of resources.

Defence agents also expressed concern that accused persons might not fully understand the role of the bail information officer. Some accused, it was said, mistook the bail officer for a member of the fiscal or police service. There was, furthermore, a risk that, because they had not seen their defence agents before being interviewed by the bail information officer, accused might not fully appreciate that unverified or negative information would be presented to the court even though the bail information officer had explained the purpose of the scheme. It was suggested that the bail information officer should carry some form of identification and should consult with defence agents before passing on information to the court.

Negative information was not in itself a problem as far as agents were concerned. Most thought that if an accused deliberately misled the bail information officer and this was discovered, then the accused only had her or himself to blame. Others, as previously indicated, sought greater involvement to protect accused who might not be fully aware that any information offered for verification would be conveyed to the court.

Views were mixed about the role of accommodation in the bail scheme. Most agents believed that few accused were in need of either hostel or other accommodation and that it was uncommon for an accused to be remanded in custody for want of an address. Others, on the other hand, considered that the lack of accommodation had resulted in unnecessary remands. Most of the defence agents were unaware of the existence of the bail accommodation scheme.

There was some limited support for hostel provision for bailees. Bail hostels were thought particularly appropriate for young people with unsettled addresses who were especially vulnerable. Associated supervision could be useful if the accused then received a probation order and continuity could, therefore, be maintained. Defence agents stressed that supervision of bailees should be provided only on a voluntary basis and only following consultation with the defence who could help to ensure that any such arrangements were in the best interests of the accused.

Glasgow defence agents

On the whole, defence agents in Glasgow were highly appreciative of the bail information service though some criticisms were expressed. The staff themselves were found to be very approachable and helpful. Several agents suggested that the visibility of the bail officers in the court had helped the scheme to become established and well-accepted.

The bail service was said to have been very successful in reducing the number of overnight remands for address checks. The bail officers had access to a wider range of accommodation resources than either the police or defence agents and could place accused through agencies such as the Hamish Allan Centre. The bail officers were also thought more likely to receive a positive response from families and parents and to be more persistent than the police in finding accommodation for accused.

There was, it was thought, a real need to locate suitable accommodation for the large number of clients without addresses who went through the court. Appropriate accommodation and support was, in particular, required for very vulnerable young people or for drug users who were often not able to sustain their own tenancies and either lived on the streets or moved frequently from address to address.

Other types of information were also of value, though to a lesser extent. Bail officers could verify whether or not accused had jobs or job interviews, comment on their family commitments or confirm how they were progressing on a community service or probation order. These were tasks which defence agents rarely had time to undertake. Some sheriffs were said to be wary of relying on unverified statements from the defence and preferred to have available an independently verified source of information. There had been many instances in which agents judged that an accused had not been remanded in custody as a result of information provided by the bail scheme.

Agents, finally, had also found bail reports useful in other circumstances. For example, they were useful in High Court appeals against remands in custody (where information contained in the bail report suggested that the accused could be bailed), in legal aid applications and at sentencing.

Some concerns were, nevertheless, expressed. Bail information reports could, it was suggested, be a double-edged sword, providing the court in some instances with information detrimental to the accused. Agents were concerned that an accused might not fully understand the purpose of the bail scheme and may, as a consequence, provide the bail officers with information (such as the existence of a drug problem) which was against their own interests. Once the information was included in a bail report the agent had no control over whether or not it should be revealed or how it should be interpreted. Because accused were contacted by bail officers before they had seen their agent, defence agents could not assist their clients in making informed decisions about the types of information to disclose. Several thought it would be helpful if defence agents could have more control over the types of information presented to the court.

One defence agent was concerned that the fiscals did not always provide the bail officers with the names of all accused for whom bail was to be opposed. Examples were provided of cases being delayed and accused being remanded overnight because bail information had not been available.

Another agent commented that the success of the scheme depended upon sheriffs being aware of and reading bail reports. It was thought that a few sheriffs confused bail information reports with social enquiry reports. Both sheriffs and fiscals were said to vary considerably in how they responded to bail reports.

There was, finally, mixed support amongst defence agents for the use of bail hostels and bail supervision. Whilst there was a need for young people in particular to receive help and support with accommodation and other problems (particularly drug use), this was not necessarily best dealt with under the aegis of bail. Most Glasgow agents thought that the Hamish Allan Centre was able to cater for young people with housing needs.

Greater importance was attached to developing a similar scheme in the district court where there was a high number of remands for less serious offences. Some agents indicated that they would also welcome the opportunity to make referrals directly to the scheme. Other areas to which the bail officers might devote greater attention included warrants, petition cases and the provision of verified information following conviction when bail was being considered pending the preparation of reports.

Summary

Interviews with the different groups revealed similar responses to those found in other studies. As outlined by Melvin and Didcott in 1976, and by Lloyd in 1992, prosecutors are primarily concerned with identifying which accused are likely to breach bail, especially those judged likely to commit offences whilst on bail. In order to form an attitude to bail, prosecutors draw almost exclusively upon the accused person's criminal record (including responses to previous periods of bail) and details of the current offence. Fiscals are key agents in the bail process: if bail is not opposed by the fiscal then it will almost invariably be granted by the courts. If bail services have the potential to remove the fiscal's grounds for opposition to bail then a custodial remand is unlikely.

The fiscals saw the relevance of bail services as primarily related to accommodation and believed that other types of information were less significant with respect to their role. At the same time it was accepted that information about community ties would be of greater use to sheriffs. Although the type of accommodation required by the accused would differ from case to case, fiscals simply required, in the majority of cases, that the court be provided with a domicile of citation. In cases involving domestic violence and in other cases involving serious offences greater assurances regarding the accused person's intended residence would be required.

Sheriffs had less contact with the bail schemes but generally were in favour of courts being provided with an independent source of verification. Examples were cited where information on the accused person's health or family situation had enabled the sheriff to allow bail to be granted. This is consistent with data presented in Chapter Five which suggested that bail information could impact positively at this stage of the bail process.

Finally, as has been found in studies in England and Wales (eg Godson and Mitchell, 1992; Lloyd, 1992) defence agents generally welcomed bail information because it helped them put forward a stronger argument in favour of bail through providing independent evidence of the circumstances of their clients.

It was clear from all groups of interviewees involved in the bail process that a credible scheme is one which is visible and understandable to all involved. It is important that court users are made aware of the existence of a report and, if it is not possible to provide reports in all bail-opposed cases, that users are made aware of the reasons behind this. The physical presence of the bail officer in the court is probably the most effective way that this can be achieved.

9 The costs of bail services

Ann Netten and Martin Knapp

Introduction

Previous chapters have identified the aims and objectives of the bail information and accommodation schemes in terms of outcomes for individuals and the criminal justice system. The resource implications of the schemes must also be considered, and this is the focus of the present chapter.

There was an expectation that the bail information and accommodation schemes might produce savings for the criminal justice system in two ways:

- through the provision of quickly available information and placements, obviating the need for overnight remands for further enquiries, and

- through the prevention of unnecessary remands in custody pending trial.

In evaluating the resource implications of the schemes it is therefore important to be aware of both their costs and the savings incurred as a result of the activities of the bail information and accommodation officers. Both costs and savings are likely to vary between the two schemes, not just because of differences in their operation, but also because of the differences in the way information was gathered and placements made. The research described in this chapter therefore includes an examination of the two schemes as well as consideration of the cost implications for the criminal justice system, in particular the relative costs of granting bail and remanding in custody.

Methodology

Broad principles

At a general level, the methodology underpinning this cost study has been built on the accepted principles of applied costs analysis (see Knapp, 1992; Netten and Beecham, editors, 1992). Costs were therefore defined and measured as comprehensively as possible, paying particular attention to the need for consistency of inclusion and treatment. This helps in the attempt to ensure that like-with-like comparisons are made between schemes and their alternatives, although because people were not randomly allocated to either bail or custody, and because the study is concentrated on just two schemes, controlling for all possible differences between them is infeasible. Costs were linked to outcomes wherever possible. Values were attached to services in accordance with the usual principle of long run marginal opportunity costing.[1] The methodology employed in this study is to try to attach costs to each of the items and routes through the criminal justice system with and without the bail information and accommodation schemes.

Time diaries

Differences in the organisation of the bail information and accommodation schemes have been described in detail in earlier chapters. In order to tease out the cost implications of these arrangements, the bail information and accommodation officers were asked to complete time diaries for one week during June 1992. These diaries detailed the time spent on various tasks and, when they contacted professional or other public employees, the bail officers specified the amount of time taken and tasks which they asked others to undertake. This, together with the worksheets and bail information reports completed during the week, gave a picture of the resources used in producing a bail information report. There was more difficulty in establishing the resources necessary to make an accommodation placement, and it was necessary to draw on the results of the main evaluation to impute a cost of finding accommodation for those on bail (see below). Consultation with the officers involved and comparison with the results of the main evaluation established that this was a sufficiently typical week for each of the schemes for the purposes of costing.

Bail scheme accounts

The 1991/92 accounts for the two schemes were used in order to attach prices to directly provided resources. The funding arrangements for the two schemes

---

[1] It would be tedious to give full details of the costing of every individual service covered by this evaluation. Details are given where appropriate, and further information is available from the authors.

differed. The Scottish Office funded both schemes, but in Glasgow it was the Regional Council which employed the bail officers whereas in Lothian it was SACRO. The accounts were presented differently, and did not include identical sets of expenditures. For example, Strathclyde Regional Council had not claimed for training expenses although it provided in-service training in the form of induction courses and a one-day course on court-related work for one of the officers. Allowance was made for this by estimating the average cost of each type of course on the basis of preparation time, accommodation and the time spent on the course itself by officers of Strathclyde Regional Council, allowing for the likely numbers of people attending each type of course. The average weekly cost of the schemes was calculated so as to ensure comparability and to facilitate the use of the time diary information.

Indirect bail scheme costs

The indirect costs of the schemes, primarily contacts with and requests made of other publicly funded employees, were built up from salary scales for relevant officials provided by Strathclyde Regional Council, the Hamish Allen Centre and the Crown Office. Proportions were added to these salaries to allow for on-costs (that is, employment costs) and overheads, and some adjustments made. For instance, in the case of social work time, the cost per minute was inflated in order to allow for the finding that 23 per cent of social worker time in Scotland is not directly client related (Tibbitt and Martin, 1991). The costs of placements in basic and supported hostel accommodation were provided by the Hamish Allen Centre and Lothian Regional Council. The costs of placements with landladies were provided by the bail accommodation officer in Edinburgh. Lothian police provided the price of a police constable's time, including allowance for overhead costs. The costs of court time and prosecution were based on earlier work of our own (Knapp and Netten, 1992) and inflated to 1991/92 levels using the implied GDP inflator (market prices).[2] The figures for legal aid were taken from the 1991/92 report of the Scottish Legal Aid Board. It was not possible to cost contacts with defence agents because of the difficulties of obtaining the necessary information; however, it can be seen elsewhere in this volume that the operation of the bail information and accommodation schemes saved defence agents a small amount of time and effort. In so far as these savings are significant, our inability to cost them results in the underestimation of the costs of custodial remands.

---

[2] Other price inflators were not available to take us up to 1991/92 levels, and would anyway have little differential effect on the costings.

The costs of bail information

The bulk of the cost of producing a bail information report is in the form of the direct cost of an information officer's time and associated overheads. In Glasgow, where the roles of accommodation finding and information gathering were combined, the use of time diaries allowed a distinction to be made between the different activities. In order to establish comparability with the Edinburgh scheme, a narrow definition of accommodation activities was taken: only those activities concerned with placements (or development of potential placements) in hostels or with landladies. Using this definition, and allowing for other activities which were not specifically related to information or accommodation work, 91 per cent of bail officers' time was found to have been spent on information gathering.

Table 9.1 contrasts the proportions of time spent on different activities in the two schemes.

Table 9.1
Bail information activities during sample week

	Percentage of time	
	Glasgow	Edinburgh
Referrals	10	16
Interviews	9	10
Enquiries	10	19
Report writing	5	5
In court	20	14
Meetings/supervision	10	6
Other[*]	36	30

[*] Includes general administration, dealing with a variety of general queries, lunch and coffee breaks and trade union activities

The organisational differences between the courts and procurator fiscal departments in Glasgow and Edinburgh resulted in a higher proportion of bail information officer time in Edinburgh being spent on referrals. The officers in Glasgow spent a higher proportion of time in court and at meetings or in supervision, and less time directly making enquiries. This is primarily due to the fact that in Glasgow more use was made of other agencies (usually the police or social work department) to establish information. In Edinburgh, the bail information officer carried out more verifications of information personally. These different patterns of working fed through into the costs of producing bail information reports.

The average weekly cost of the information element of the schemes was £840 in Glasgow and £567 in Edinburgh. These costs allow for clerical assistance, overheads, training and travel, and include the cost of direct supervision time by the Assistant District Officer in Glasgow.[3] For the purposes of comparison, it is most helpful to examine the cost per unit of output, that is per bail information report.

Table 9.2 gives the numbers of reports, both verbal and written, together with investigations resulting in no report, during the sample week in which the time diaries were completed.

Table 9.2
Information reports during sample week

	Glasgow	Edinburgh
Written reports	23	13
Verbal reports	4	1
Investigation but no report	8	2

In both Glasgow and Edinburgh there were more referrals than could be dealt with by the officers. In Glasgow the procurators fiscal identified four cases that could not be interviewed due to pressure of work. In Edinburgh the procurators fiscal identified ten cases, and the bail information officer a further ten cases that he considered would have benefited from a report.

Using the figures for output in Table 9.2 (27 reports in Glasgow and 14 in Edinburgh), the average direct cost of producing a report was £31 in Glasgow and £41 in Edinburgh. The main reason for the disparity is salary levels and the higher level of travel-related expenditure in Edinburgh: the officer received

---

[3] Both schemes had advisory groups, the Edinburgh group met during the week of the time diary study. In principle, the costs of these advisory groups should be included in a fully comprehensive measure, but for the purposes of this evaluation they can be ignored since the equivalent high level management of custodial remands were not included here. In fact the costs of advisory group meetings would be very small when set alongside other expenditures, as the groups met every three months, each meeting lasting two or three hours.

an essential car user's allowance. There was also more training expenditure in Edinburgh than Glasgow. However, the training expenditure was more than offset by the estimated cost of direct supervision which, on the basis of the direct time involvement reported in the time diaries, contributed an additional £941 each year to the cost of bail information in Glasgow. Clearly, however, differences in the mode of working meant that the Glasgow scheme was likely to incur higher indirect costs in establishing information. Table 9.3 shows the average number of minutes per week of contact with professionals and other public employees.

Table 9.3
Time spent by others on bail information reports

| | Number of minutes per report | |
	Glasgow	Edinburgh
Social workers	9.82	3.45
Police	8.33	0.36
Procurators fiscal	3.11	3.64
Other	2.41	1.29
Total	23.67	8.74

Earlier chapters have established that most verification was obtained from professionals working in various agencies. Where contacts were made with family members or friends, these could involve a great deal of time.

In identifying the amount of time spent by others as a result of contacts made by bail information officers, it has been assumed that every contact resulted in at least five minutes work. This was to allow for the effect of interruptions, however short an individual telephone call may have been. The amount of time spent by the procurators fiscal in Glasgow was enhanced by 20 per cent to allow for time spent trying unsuccessfully to contact bail information officers. In Edinburgh, a further 26 minutes was added to the direct contact time of procurators fiscal with the bail information officer; this allowed a minute for the addition of each report to the list to be referred to the bail scheme. In interview fiscals in Glasgow were of the opinion that a referral system such as that used in Edinburgh would be more efficient. This was discussed with the bail officers and a joint decision made to retain the system of referring cases as they were marked as bail being opposed. In fact the amount of time the fiscals spent on each case was lower under the Glasgow system of referral than under that adopted in Edinburgh.

The commitments of time reported in Table 9.3 include time spent as a result of contacts: five police officers and one social worker carried out address checks at the request of the information officers in Glasgow. Table 9.4 converts these time commitments into costs per report.

Table 9.4
Indirect costs of producing bail information reports

	Cost per report (£)	
	Glasgow	Edinburgh
Social workers	1.73	0.61
Police	2.93	0.13
Procurators fiscal	1.23	1.49
Other	0.33	0.17
Total	6.27	2.40

Many short contacts with people from a number of different agencies are included in the 'other' category. Contacts with hostel workers - which were the largest single group in this category - were costed separately. Otherwise, contact was costed at the level of a clerical officer.[4] Adding these indirect costs to the direct costs demonstrates that the cost of producing a report in Edinburgh (£43) is still higher than in Glasgow (£37), although the difference is small.[5]

---

[4] Even with the vast expansion of these schemes, the time implications of contacts for the various agencies would be small. The short run and long run marginal costs of these contacts are likely to be similar, and are most likely to be felt in terms of clerical staff time.

[5] This cost does not allow for the use of interview rooms, normally attached to cells where prisoners were held prior to court hearings. (For information, the time use was 234 minutes per week in Edinburgh, and 338 minutes per week in Glasgow.) These costs amount to just a few pence per case, although any marked expansion of the schemes would put considerable pressure on available capacity during peak periods, and might require additional facilities to be erected.

The costs of accommodation placements

There are three elements to be included in the costing of accommodation: the accommodation itself, the resources of the two schemes devoted to developing and securing accommodation (consisting primarily of the time spent by the bail accommodation officers) and the various indirect costs. The costs of the accommodation itself are considered below. Unfortunately, calculation of the other two costs - which together comprise the cost of *making* accommodation placements - presented difficulties. The operational problems associated with the accommodation activities of the schemes have been discussed in earlier chapters. The bail officers spent time on general development as well as on specific referrals, which itself generates research problems over and above the operational considerations. As identified above, in Glasgow a total of nine per cent of bail officers' time was spent on accommodation (using a narrow definition of the term). In Edinburgh, one officer was employed full time to deal with accommodation issues. In Glasgow, 59 per cent of bail officers' time spent on specific accommodation-related tasks was devoted to the developmental side of the schemes. Time distribution data were not available for the accommodation element of the Edinburgh scheme. These distributions of time caused the average weekly costs of the accommodation element to differ considerably: £83 per week in Glasgow and £357 per week in Edinburgh. In addition, a placement in a hostel in Glasgow involved referral via the Hamish Allen Centre, for which a cost of £5 has been allowed. In Edinburgh, £160 was spent on publicity and advertisements during the year, which gives an additional cost of £3 per week. Further costs would be incurred by other agencies in the process of developing and securing accommodation places.

These costs are likely to be very modest, but we did not have sufficient data on which to base an accurate assessment. Although hostels and the Hamish Allen Centre in Glasgow were aware of the schemes and nominally set beds aside, these would not be kept empty if there were other referrals, and so there were no opportunity costs associated with empty beds. In the Edinburgh accounts, on the other hand, £519 was declared paid to landladies during 1991/92 to retain beds. In practice these payments were largely to compensate landladies when rent was not paid either by the individual or the DSS. In either case allowance should be made for this in the costing of placements. These costs have therefore been added to the weekly costs of a landlady placement (see below).

As we argued in relation to the costs of the information activity, it is important to link costs to outputs when comparing the two schemes. This causes some difficulty, for there are at least four alternative definitions of outcome:

- the number of successful accommodation placements (for whom a placement was found and who were released on bail);

- the number of people for whom each scheme negotiated accommodation and produced a report for the court;

- the number of referrals for accommodation, whether or not successful; and

- the total number of people with whom a scheme worked, for in principle the accommodation placement facility was available to them all, and development work could have benefited them all.[6]

Moreover, although there might be arguments to favour one outcome measure over another, the objectives of the two schemes ranged across all four of the activities reflected in these outcomes - from general development to successful placement - and the early stages of operation meant the uneven progress of these activities. To compound the research difficulties, measures were not easy to obtain. During the week that the officers completed time diaries neither scheme made a successful accommodation placement. In Glasgow one referral was made and a hostel place found but the individual was remanded in custody. In Edinburgh, there were four referrals, three from the bail information officer and one from a social worker. In one case a place was found but again the court remanded the individual in custody. In one instance the referral was diverted from prosecution and in another the hostel refused because of past violent behaviour. The last referral proved impossible to place as he was too old for one hostel, the other hostel was full and previous convictions for sexual offences meant he was unsuitable to be placed with a landlady.

Other data collected over the duration of the schemes provide estimates of the outcome measures identified above. The Glasgow and Edinburgh schemes were monitored for five and nine months respectively. During these periods there were:

- 28 bailees offered accommodation in Glasgow and 17 in Edinburgh;

- 67 reports offering accommodation in Glasgow and 46 in Edinburgh;

---

[6] In the manner of an option demand benefit.

136

- 98 referrals for accommodation in Glasgow and 62 in Edinburgh;

- 418 cases dealt with in Glasgow and 553 people in Edinburgh.

Using these different outcome measures to generate alternative average cost measures implies that the average cost of a successful placement was £69 in Glasgow and £819 in Edinburgh. In terms of reports submitted, the average cost of accommodation placement was £32 per report in Glasgow and £305 per report in Edinburgh. Using referrals as a basis for comparison, each referral in Glasgow cost £23 compared with £227 in Edinburgh. Finally, accepting the argument that the schemes could potentially have offered a service to *all* referrals, the cost for each referral was £25 in Edinburgh and, assuming three approaches each week to the Hamish Allen Centre, £5 per referral in Glasgow.

Clearly, the difficulties encountered in developing the accommodation side of the schemes (which are discussed elsewhere in this report) largely account for the difference in costs between Edinburgh and Glasgow. It is worth noting, however, that the structure of the two schemes meant that difficulties with the accommodation side of the work in Glasgow resulted in the majority of the available time being devoted to the production of bail information reports. Although there was clearly excess demand for information reports in Edinburgh (see above), the separation of the two roles on two different sites meant that this option was not open to the officers concerned. Thus the spare capacity in the accommodation side of the schemes is reflected in much higher costs for each measurable output.

These bail information and accommodation costs will be used below to pull together the costs of different routes through the criminal justice system. These routes are summarised in Table 9.5. For simplicity, cases which plead guilty at the pleading diet are excluded from the set of options considered. It can reasonably be assumed (a) that no further costs are incurred other than the sentence received, and (b) that since bail information officers did not discuss the offence or plea with the accused, the likelihood of pleading guilty at this stage is the same for those who are the subject of a bail information report and those who are not. When reporting the costs, the operational difficulties faced by the Edinburgh scheme in relation to accommodation placements make it prudent to concentrate on the Glasgow scheme, whose full costs will be reported in Table 9.6.

Table 9.5
Routes through the system

Route[1]	Bail scheme[2]	RIC overnight[3]	Court decision[4]	Breach[5]	Trial sentence[6]
1	I		Bail		C
2	I		Bail		N-C
3	I		Bail		NG
4	I		Bail	Yes	C
5	I		Bail	Yes	N-C
6	I		Bail	Yes	NG
7	I		RIC		C
8	I		RIC		N-C
9	I		RIC		NG
10	IA		Bail		C
11	IA		Bail		N-C
12	IA		Bail		NG
13	IA		Bail	Yes	C
14	IA		Bail	Yes	N-C
15	IA		Bail	Yes	NG
16	IA		RIC		C
17	IA		RIC		N-C
18	IA		RIC		NG
19			Bail		C
20			Bail		N-C
21			Bail		NG
22			Bail	Yes	C
23			Bail	Yes	N-C
24			Bail	Yes	NG
25			RIC		C
26			RIC		N-C
27			RIC		NG
28		Yes	Bail		C
29		Yes	Bail		N-C
30		Yes	Bail		NG
31		Yes	Bail	Yes	C
32		Yes	Bail	Yes	N-C
33		Yes	Bail	Yes	NG
34		Yes	RIC		C
35		Yes	RIC		N-C
36		Yes	RIC		NG

Notes: 1. Routes 1-18 go through the schemes. Routes 10-18 involve both information and accommodation, and routes 1-9 only the former. Routes 19-36 do *not* go through the schemes: routes 28-36 involve an overnight remand for more information
2. Bail scheme services received: information (I) and accommodation (A)
3. Whether remanded into custody overnight after initial appearance in court (for more information)
4. Decision at pleading diet
5. Breach of bail
6. Trial verdict and sentence: custody (C), non-custodial (N-C), not guilty (NG)

Costs of court appearances and overnight remands in custody

After completion of the information report, the next stage is the court appearance, which of course occurs whether or not there has been any activity by the bail officers. However, the cost consequences depend upon whether there has been any such activity. The most important contribution to this variation is the cost of overnight remands in custody. Of lesser importance quantitatively, but not to be overlooked, are the direct and indirect costs associated with any differences in court time, particularly a second court appearance, and also any time spent by the police or others in obtaining information.

Time spent in court

What were the effects of verified information and placements on the time spent in court at each appearance? The observation of court procedures was described in Chapter One. This identified that, when bail was opposed and reference made to a bail report, cases took on average 3.2 minutes less in Glasgow and 2 minutes less in Edinburgh than they would have done in the absence of a report. This results in a £19 saving in court time in Glasgow and a saving in Edinburgh of £11 for each case where a bail report is available . Table 9.6 shows the consequences for total cost of a pleading diet for each path for cases in Glasgow. It was assumed that all cases received legal aid which for serious crime, theft and other crime is £48 per case (Scottish Legal Aid Board, 1992).

Overnight remands

Overnight remands in prison cells were costed using figures reported in *Prisons in Scotland* (Scottish Office, 1991). These average costs include transport but do not distinguish types of prison or prisoner. However, data on English prisons reveals that the average costs of remand and local prisons are almost the same as the overall average prison cost (see, for example, *Report on the Work of the Prison Service*, Home Office, 1991).[7] Inflating Scottish prison revenue costs (£23,899 per prisoner year, 1990/92) to 1991/92 price

---

[7] Previous research on variations in the costs of custody among English prisons allowed costs to be associated with inmate characteristics, including security rating and remand status (Knapp and Fenyo, 1988). In costing overnight remands, there is insufficient evidence in the present study to utilise fully the cost function estimates obtained in that earlier work, though we have used these estimates to cost custodial sentences.

Table 9.6
Total costs per case in Glasgow by route through the system

Route	Bail scheme £	Court appearance £	RIC overnight £	Bail £	RIC £	Breach of bail £	Sentence £	Total £
1	37	91	-	689	-	-	4713	5530
2	37	91	-	689	-	-	968	1785
3	37	91	-	689	-	-	-	817
4	37	91	-	689	-	1220	4713	6750
5	37	91	-	689	-	1220	968	3005
6	37	91	-	689	-	1220	-	2037
7	37	91	-	-	1510	-	3858	5496
8	37	91	-	-	1510	-	968	2606
9	37	91	-	-	1510	-	-	1638
10	69	91	-	689	-	-	4713	5562
11	69	91	-	689	-	-	968	1817
12	69	91	-	689	-	-	-	849
13	69	91	-	689	-	1220	4713	6782
14	69	91	-	689	-	1220	968	3037
15	69	91	-	689	-	1220	-	2069
16	69	91	-	-	1510	-	3858	5528
17	69	91	-	-	1510	-	968	2638
18	69	91	-	-	1510	-	-	1670
19	-	110	-	520	-	-	4713	5343
20	-	110	-	520	-	-	968	1598
21	-	110	-	520	-	-	-	630
22	-	110	-	520	-	1220	4713	6563
23	-	110	-	520	-	1220	968	2818
24	-	110	-	520	-	1220	-	1850
25	-	110	-	-	1510	-	3858	5478
26	-	110	-	-	1510	-	968	2588
27	-	110	-	-	1510	-	-	1620
28	-	110	186	520	-	-	4713	5529
29	-	110	186	520	-	-	968	1784
30	-	110	186	520	-	-	-	816
31	-	110	186	520	-	1220	4713	6749
32	-	110	186	520	-	1220	968	3004
33	-	110	186	520	-	1220	-	2036
34	-	110	186	-	1510	-	3858	5664
35	-	110	186	-	1510	-	968	2774
36	-	110	186	-	1510	-	-	1806

levels using the inflation implicit in a recent Scottish Office (1992b) report, and adding a capital cost element based on a Parliamentary Answer in December 1988 concerning the costs of new prisons, gives the full cost per day as £89. Since 'overnight' remands can actually last all or part of the weekend, a more accurate figure for the average cost of an overnight remand is £128.

Obtaining information

When the accused has been remanded overnight in order to establish a home address or to check other information, there will be an additional cost. This cost would include the direct time of the officials involved, who would normally be social workers and/or police officers. Allowing thirty minutes of social work time and thirty minutes of police time for establishing information would suggest a cost of approximately £16 for an enquiry. In addition, there would be a further court appearance which - assuming it takes the same time as a case where there is a bail information report, that 90 per cent of the procurator fiscal preparation costs are necessary, and assuming that no further legal aid costs were incurred - would imply an additional cost of £42 per case.

Comparative costs thus far

The implications of the bail information and accommodation schemes have not yet been fully costed, but it is interesting to compare the costs of the main routes thus far.[8] The costs reported in the first three columns of Table 9.6 have now been obtained. Recall that these costs are confined to the Glasgow scheme. (A similar table could be drawn up for Edinburgh, though operational difficulties make this problematic at this stage.) The typical recipient of bail information (only) in Glasgow cost £128 (see lines 1 to 9 in Table 9.6), and the typical recipient of bail information *and* accommodation (that is the additional cost of producing evidence about formal accommodation in a report) cost £160 (lines 10 to 18). In contrast, the estimated average cost of an overnight remand is £296 (lines 28 to 36). Excluding the cost of the initial court appearance and accommodation, the cost of obtaining information by remanding an individual in custody overnight (£186) represents the cost of about five information reports. Thus the bail information scheme would represent a saving at this stage if more than one in five of these borderline

---

[8] In principle, it would be expected better information and improved decision making would reduce the number of appeals. There is no information on this possibility in the present study, and so appeals are not costed here.

cases would have been remanded overnight for an address check.

The costs of bail

The costs of being released on bail consist primarily of the costs of accommodation, income support payments and services received. In addition to these basic costs are the resource implications of a breach of bail. In comparing the costs of remands in custody with the costs of bail it is important to take account of differences in the duration of time spent on the two alternatives. Cases on bail take longer to come to court: in the two schemes, the average length of time between the pleading diet and trial date was 13 weeks for those on bail and three weeks for those in custodial remand.

Accommodation placements

A variety of accommodation placements was available across the two schemes. Table 9.7 sets out the average weekly cost of each of these.

Table 9.7
Average weekly costs of accommodation

	Average weekly cost (£)	
	Excluding DSS payments	Including DSS expenditure
Allalon	356	378
Albrae	266	277
Hamish Allen Centre Hostel	73	119[1]
Landlady	64	98[1]
Private households	-	52[2]

[1] Assumes average weekly income support of £49
[2] Assumes average weekly income support including housing benefit of £52

Allalon and Albrae were considerably more expensive than the other placements because they provide all meals and staff support. The type of hostel place provided by the Hamish Allen Centre, on the other hand, only supplied breakfast and (officially) no counselling or staff support (although all homeless people were interviewed by a senior caseworker to discuss their housing needs). For the most part, landladies recruited to the scheme in Edinburgh charged £50 each week and provided no meals. One landlady placement used during the scheme provided all food and extra support for £165 each week, but this was exceptional, and it proved impossible to claim housing benefit at an appropriate rate, so that the place was withdrawn from the scheme. The additional cost of £14 per week (in Table 9.7) reflects the money paid to landladies to compensate them for non-payment by bailees. There were two placements with landladies over the nine month monitoring period which accounted for three-quarters of the £519 paid to landladies during the year.

The average weekly cost of an accommodation placement to the state depends upon income support and housing benefit payments. In all cases where people are placed in hostels or with landladies they are in receipt of such benefits; otherwise they are not accepted. In Allalon and Albrae, these benefits pay for the hostel placement and individuals receive a small personal allowance. In Hamish Allen Centre hostels, a minimum contribution of £3.50 per week is expected from individuals and the remainder of the hostel placement cost is claimed as housing benefit. The individual retains other income support payments such as sickness benefit. Similarly, individuals pay £15 towards a landlady place and £35 is provided by housing benefit.

The second column in Table 9.7 shows the cost of placement assuming that the individual is in receipt of income support. For private households it is assumed that the level of income support was the average for those cases who received bail during the week in which bail officers completed time diaries, including the single case where the receipt of housing benefit was identified. The average level of benefit excluding this case was used to illustrate the total cost of a placement with landladies or in a Hamish Allen Centre hostel place.

In allocating an appropriate estimated cost it is necessary to be clear about both the probability that an individual in a private household will be receiving benefits and the proportion of people in each type of placement. Earlier chapters reported that 78 per cent of referrals in Glasgow were unemployed. Assuming that a similar proportion to those in Edinburgh are in receipt of benefits (82 per cent), this means that 62 per cent of the cases in Glasgow would be receiving benefits. During the monitoring period only 32 people or 17 per cent of cases in Glasgow were in a hostel whilst on bail. Using this as a basis, the average weekly accommodation and DSS cost as a result of an individual being on bail in Glasgow was £47. Four of these people were in a hostel prior to their arrest so it was assumed that in the absence of the schemes just two per cent would have been in hostels. In this case the cost would be

£34 per week.

Social work involvement

When comparing the costs of bail with the costs of remands in custody (set out in detail below), it is necessary to consider the impact of services received in the community that would not be received in prison, or that would be included in prison costs. The only service that was in widespread use by those on bail was social work involvement of one form or another. The problem in deciding the impact of the bail or custody decision on social work involvement is that a number of factors will influence whether involvement will increase or decrease. If the case is coming towards the end of a probation order then a custody decision will probably result in a decrease in involvement by a social worker (one visit per month would change from being the minimum to the maximum, though any visits made will now probably take longer and will involve travelling time and expenses). If the case concerns a young person in custody for the first time or if there is a social enquiry report to be prepared, then the social work time associated with the case would increase as a result of a custody decision. The severity of the case and child care issues will also affect the level of involvement. In the absence of detailed information on these various factors, it is not possible to be clear as to the 'average' level of commitment of a social worker to a bail case or a case remanded in custody. For the purposes of costing, it has therefore been assumed that receipt averages one hour per fortnight. Of the 16 cases for whom information was available, five were in contact with the social work department. This was equivalent to a weekly cost of £2 for the full sample.

Community service orders

A proportion of those on bail were also serving community service orders. The number of community service hours ordered will have to be served even though the individual is remanded in custody, and the orders themselves are not connected with the alleged offence which produced the bail decision, so no additional costs need to be attributed to those on bail.

Health services

The only other services received by the 16 cases on bail for which information was available during the time diary week were health services. Three bailees were taking medication such as anti-depressants and four were clearly in regular contact with their GP. A psychiatrist was involved in one case and a community psychiatric nurse in another. Assuming fortnightly contacts with the GP and CPN, and monthly consultations with the psychiatrist, average weekly costs across the full sample amount to £4.

The full costs of bail

Table 9.6 summarises these calculations, reporting that the average cost per case of the period on bail is estimated as £689 when the schemes were operating and £520 in the absence of the schemes.

The costs of breaching bail

A major concern about bail is the possibility of breach, whether non-appearance at court or further offences, including violation of any special conditions attached to bail orders. These have been discussed at length elsewhere in this volume, where it was shown that 90 per cent of breaches resulted from further offences. These breaches need to be costed.

Breach costs - non-appearance

The cost of non-appearance can be estimated on the same basis as in an earlier study (Knapp and Netten, 1992). Police time amounting to 3.5 hours is assumed necessary in order to serve the warrant (£74). This is less than the time allowed in our earlier study, but reflects the fact that the hourly cost used here allows for the impact of administrative tasks and other overheads. The preparation and court time required for the hearing at which the accused did not appear also need to be included. Assuming the case takes two minutes of court time, this adds a further £40 to the cost of a breach.

Breach costs - further offences

The resource implications of committing further offences while on bail include the costs of the offence itself, the cost of preparing the case for the procurator fiscal, the cost of overnight remands in police cells, and the costs of prosecution and sentence. It is very difficult to measure the social costs of offences, but estimates may be substituted from a 1989 study in Northumbria. This study found that 4915 offences had been committed by 695 bailees in one area, at a total social cost of £1.8 million.[9] Using these figures the social cost per offender would be estimated at £2,972 (at 1991/92 prices). In Table 9.6 however, we have focused on the costs to the criminal justice system.

The cost of investigating a case and preparing a brief report for the procurator fiscal will vary widely between cases. So far as we are aware there are no estimates of the amount of police time involved and the assumption has been made that six hours of police time are involved, the cost of which would be £127. It is assumed that all breach of bail cases that had been the subject of debate over whether they should be remanded in custody for the offence for which they were granted bail would be detained overnight in police cells before the pleading diet. There is no information available about the costs of detention in police cells in Scotland. The average weekly cost of remands in police cells in England was estimated by NACRO as £651 in 1986/87. Assuming the costs in Scotland are the same and inflating this to 1991/92 levels (allowing for courts sitting five days per week) results in an estimated cost of £182 for overnight detentions for each case.

In Scotland breach of bail cases have to be prosecuted separately to the initial offence. Assuming that these cases are the same as the cases seen by the scheme as a whole then 12 per cent are likely to plead guilty at the pleading diet. Making the assumption that, of those who plead not guilty at the pleading diet, the proportion who plead guilty at trial is the same as for sheriff court cases as a whole, a further 64 per cent will plead guilty at the trial diet. Using these proportions and adjusting the price base of Knapp and Netten's (1992) costs of prosecution results in an average cost of £669.

An allowance for legal aid needs to be added. As pointed out above, people detained in custody are entitled to automatic legal aid before they have pled. The majority will receive normal advice and assistance, but those who plead guilty at the pleading diet will be entitled to advice by way of representation (ABWOR). It was assumed that the same proportion received this type of legal aid in the two areas covered by the evaluation as in Scotland as a whole for crime and theft cases, giving average legal aid costs of £54. To this needs to be added the full legal aid costs of those who initially plead not guilty, but it is difficult to assess the probability that individuals will receive full legal aid. Approximately two thirds of cases are in receipt of income support and clearly entitled to receive legal aid, but the Scottish Legal Aid Board's (1992) report

---

[9] Correspondence with Jim Lillie, Northumbria Police, following presentation of a paper at the Police Superintendents' Association conference, Torquay, September 1991, based on work undertaken in conjunction with researchers at Newcastle University. Costings of offences were based on figures presented by the Home Office (1988) and a local consultation document published by the Chief Constable of the Northumbria Police Force.

warns that average costs 'should be approached with caution as experience has shown that a single trial or appeal of great complexity and/or length can distort the figures'. In order to allow for this it was assumed that just half of those who pled not guilty at the pleading diet received the average level of legal aid in sheriff courts (£707). Making these assumptions and allowing for advice and assistance results in a total estimated legal aid cost for breaches of £365. It should be stressed that this is only an approximation and there is no way at present of estimating the true cost of legal aid for such cases.

The total cost of breaching bail by committing a further offence, excluding the social costs of the offence itself, are estimated on this basis as £1343. Assuming the same costs are incurred if the offence is violating bail conditions, and that 10 per cent of cases breach by failing to appear in court, results in a cost of £1,220 for breach of bail (see Table 9.6). Note that only *one* breach of bail conditions is assumed for these calculations.

Remands in custody

The costs of a remand in custody pending trial can be calculated in the same way as the costs of overnight remands, though there will now also be some social work department involvement (in the absence of other information, estimated to be the same time input as for those people on bail). Based on figures reported in *Prisons in Scotland* (Scottish Office, 1991), with the addition of a capital element, the daily custody costs are £89 (see above). Average time in custody was just over two weeks in Glasgow. This gives a total cost for the remand period of £1510.

Although the weekly costs of being maintained in a Hamish Allan Centre hostel (£125 including services) are considerably lower than being remanded in custody (£623) the length of time before the court hearing reduces the cost differential of the two paths. So while the weekly cost of remand is over five times that of the hostel placement, once the pre-trial period is allowed for a hostel placement *exceeds* the cost of being remanded in custody (£1625 compared with £1510 in prison).

Sentence costs

Sentence costs vary in response to a number of factors, particularly the type of sentence and seriousness of offence. In this cost study, it was important to recognise the differential impact on the post-trial sentence costs of an earlier remand into custody. Other influences on cost were either irrelevant or could

147

not be controlled for. It has therefore been assumed that trials produced three outcomes. In order to illustrate the effects of different routes to trial, the same three outcomes are used for all costings:

Not guilty verdict

The associated sentence costs are zero.

Non-custodial sentence

It is assumed that the non-custodial sentence is a community service (CS) order. This has been costed on the basis of an earlier study of CS (Knapp et al., 1992). The cost in Glasgow was £968, including both direct and indirect cost elements, for the average length CS order in Glasgow in 1987/88. The implied GDP inflator is used to inflate to 1991/92 price levels. This cost includes the likelihood of breach (11.5 per cent).

Custodial sentence

A custodial sentence of 140 days is assumed (with one third remission), this being the comparator used in the earlier costing of community service in Glasgow. This was the mean sentence length for people considered suitable for CS who were in fact given custodial sentences. This assumption gives an effective sentence cost of £4713. Basic revenue costs were taken from Scottish Office (1991), at £23,899 per prisoner year, at 1990/91 prices. These need to be inflated, a capital cost element added, and indirect costs estimated. Lost productivity costs are not included, but it is necessary to reduce the custody costs for savings in accommodation, food and clothing in prison. These latter are estimated from Family Expenditure Survey data. Prison costs are also adjusted to take account of the type of offence typically committed by offenders given community service orders. The result of these various calculations, which are intended to give comprehensive, consistent and comparable figures is to produce an estimate of £4713 per sentence, or £51 per day. (The full rationalisation and details are given in Knapp et al., 1992.) Note that the costs of imprisonment for people under sentence (with the exception of the highest security category) are lower than the costs for people on remand (Knapp and Fenyo, 1988).

The costs for the first and second are assumed to be invariant with respect to the routes through the criminal justice system. (They *are* correlated with the bail/RIC distinction, but it is being assumed on the basis of the data presented in Chapter Seven that this is due to the characteristics of the people and the alleged offences, rather than the effect of bail or RIC itself.) The cost of custody, which is expressed at 1991/92 prices and includes indirect as well as direct resource consequences, will be lower for those people who were remanded in custody before their trial, other things being equal. This adjustment has been made in the figures reported in Table 9.6.

The 1980 Act outlines the penalty for breach of bail; these are a fine of up to £200 and a sentence of up to three months imprisonment (for sheriff court cases). Where the accused is given a non-custodial sentence a fine will generally be imposed. Where a custodial sentence is passed, the extra sanctions of breach of bail can be imposed either to run concurrently or consecutively. Anecdotal evidence suggests that such sentences are usually concurrent with any other period of imprisonment imposed by the court. Therefore there are no additional costs associated with sentences for breach of bail.

Discussion

This chapter has reported comprehensive costings for the main resource elements associated with a number of routes through the criminal justice system. Table 9.6 pulls all of these costs together; the routes are given in Table 9.5. Before examining the impact of the probabilities of these routes on the expected costs it is of interest to contrast the routes themselves. From the costs in the final column of Table 9.6 two particular conclusions can be drawn.

The first conclusion from this cost study is that the bail information and accommodation schemes do not result in less costly outcomes than overnight remands into custody. If the first court appearance (pleading diet) results in bail which is not breached, and a verdict of not guilty is given at the trial, the costs will be as follows:

- bail information only (Route 3)   £817

- bail information and accommodation (Route 12)   £849

- remand in custody (Route 30)   £816

The reason that the figures are so similar is that the higher proportion of people in hostels as a result of schemes raises the cost of the bail period by almost as much as the cost of an overnight remand. Or compare the costs if someone is remanded in custody after the pleading diet and subsequently is given a custodial sentence:

- bail information only (Route 7)   £5496

- bail information and accommodation (Route 16)   £5528

- remand in custody (Route 34)   £5664

Generally, the four blocks of routes in Tables 9.5 and 9.6 (routes 1 to 9, 10 to 18, 19 to 27, and 28 to 36) can be compared for the various bail-remand-breach-sentence alternatives.

A second conclusion to pull out from the results in this chapter is that costs will be marginally lower without the bail information and accommodation schemes if the accused is not remanded into custody overnight. The equivalent costs of this option for comparison with the two specific examples above are £630 and £5478, or compare the third block of routes with the first and second blocks.

Table 9.8 shows the overall cost implications of the bail scheme in Glasgow.

Table 9.8
The cost implications of the bail scheme in Glasgow

	BIA Scheme £ per case	No. BIA Scheme £ per case
Bail report	42	-
Court appearance	91	110
Overnight RIC	0	7
Pre-trial period	935	847
Bail breach	205	196
Sentence	1896	1912
Total	3169	3072

This assumes that the probability of informal accommodation information in the bail information report is .16; of overnight remand when no report is .04; of bail when there is a report is .70; when no report .67; of breaching bail is .24; when bailed of custodial sentence .23; of non custodial sentence .67; of not guilty .10; when remanded in custody of custodial sentence .49; of non-custodial sentence .40 and of not guilty .11.

As Table 9.8 shows, the presence of the bail scheme in Glasgow was associated with extra costs averaging at about £100 per case. Whilst the average costs of court time, of an overnight remand in custody and of a custodial outcome were reduced by the availability of a bail scheme other costs increased. The costs associated with bail were greater than those associated with a custodial remand pending trial because time on bail was longer than a custodial remand and the scheme increased the proportion of people on bail and using hostel accommodation. Similarly, the presence of a bail scheme meant an increase in cost of breach of bail, not because people were more likely to breach their bail orders but because a slightly higher proportion of accused were bailed as a result of the bail information scheme.

The introduction of the bail information and accommodation schemes in Glasgow and in Edinburgh (where the costs were even higher) has not, therefore, resulted in appreciable cost savings to the criminal justice system. The cost analysis does allow an examination of where the costs fall and thus where costs may be reduced. For example, changes in procedures, such as shortening the period of bail for those accommodated in hostels, would result in savings. Moreover, other agencies (such as fiscals and sheriffs) have highlighted the contribution of bail information to enhancing the quality of decision-making in relation to the granting of bail. This is an additional benefit of the bail service to which a financial value cannot readily be attached.

10   Conclusions and discussion

Introduction

The research described in this volume focused on the work of two experimental bail schemes based in Edinburgh and Glasgow. This final chapter deals with two main issues. Firstly, the extent to which the schemes fulfilled their objectives (with reference to the factors which were related to effectiveness) and, secondly, the wider implications of the research findings for the development of bail services and for considerations of the bail process in general.

Achievement of objectives

An over-arching objective of both schemes was to reduce the number of unnecessary custodial remands through the provision of verified information to the courts. The schemes also aimed to locate accommodation for accused who were of no fixed abode or for whom an alternative address was required. In Edinburgh, consistent with the decision to include unverified and negative information in reports, the original objective was superseded by a concern to improve the quality of bail decisions by the court. The Edinburgh scheme aimed, in addition, to explore the feasibility of introducing bail supervision services. The extent to which these objectives were achieved are discussed in turn.

Reducing the number of remands in custody

An analysis of bail/remand outcomes among accused who were interviewed by the bail officers, along with feedback from sheriffs in individual cases, suggested that in both schemes the provision of positive verified information had resulted in the granting of bail to accused persons who would otherwise have been remanded in custody (either overnight or pending a further appearance). It was estimated that positive verified information had been instrumental in facilitating the granting of bail to approximately 19% of those who were interviewed by the bail officer in Edinburgh and 29% of those who were interviewed in Glasgow.

Assessed against the total volume of cases dealt with by the custody courts in both cities, however, bail information appeared to have had little, if any, impact upon the relative use of bail and custodial remands. Indeed an increase in the use of bail in conjunction with a decrease in the proportions of accused persons ordained to appear suggests that some net-widening may have occurred following the introduction of bail services in Edinburgh.

The apparently greater impact of bail information in Glasgow was consistent with views of procurators fiscal, sheriffs and defence agents in Edinburgh who believed that bail information reports had had a limited impact upon the bail decisions reached by the court. A number of factors appear to have contributed to the increased effectiveness of bail information in Glasgow.

In Glasgow, with the exception of a few cases referred to the scheme in court, all accused who were interviewed had been identified by the marking fiscals as those for whom the granting of bail would be opposed in court. By contrast, the bail information officer in Edinburgh was required to anticipate in advance in which cases bail was likely to be opposed by the fiscals prior to the list of bail opposed cases being made available. Whilst the targeting of cases by the bail information officer was reported to have improved over time, some accused were interviewed for whom fiscals had a favourable attitude towards the granting of bail.

Bail information could have an impact in Glasgow at two points in the bail process: when fiscals were forming an attitude towards the granting of bail and when sheriffs were considering the arguments put forward by the fiscal and by defence agents in bail opposed cases. Glasgow fiscals were willing, for example, to review their opposition to bail in court if bail was being opposed on the basis of the accused person's lack of a fixed or appropriate address and the bail scheme was able to provide verification that an address had been found. In Edinburgh, on the other hand, bail was less likely to be opposed on the basis of the lack of a fixed address and the potential impact of bail information reports was primarily at the point at which the sheriff was considering the arguments against and in favour of bail.

The availability of emergency accommodation in Glasgow also meant that most accused who were without an address and who could not be accommodated with relatives or friends could be offered immediate alternative provision. In Edinburgh the range of existing accommodation was more limited and other additional resources proved difficult to develop and sustain.

The flexibility of staff in Glasgow to move between information and accommodation roles (and to concentrate in the fist instance on the information service) meant that most accused referred by the fiscals could be interviewed and information checked prior to their court appearance. At least one bail officer was in a position to attend the court diet in the afternoon. The bail officer in Edinburgh was often unable, because of the referral process and the earlier timing of the custody court, to interview all accused whose bail was being opposed and provide verified information to the court. Nor was he in a position regularly to attend the custody court diet.

The presence in court of the bail officers in Glasgow ensured that reports were circulated, that the scheme had a high profile among court personnel and that bail staff were at hand to respond to any requests for additional information relevant to the bail decision in individual cases. In Edinburgh bail reports were not always circulated in court and the lack on a regular basis of the bail information officer in court limited the ability of sheriffs and defence agents to make referrals to the scheme.

Finally, fiscals in Glasgow appeared from the outset to have a greater sense of ownership of the bail service and this no doubt contributed to the acceptance and credibility of the scheme. Fiscals were active participants in the development of the bail scheme, appeared sympathetic to its objectives and co-operated fully in ensuring that appropriate cases were referred. Edinburgh fiscals, however, were doubtful from the outset about the value of bail information and the impact that such a scheme might have. This was reflected, in turn, in the less direct involvement of Edinburgh fiscals in the day to day operation of the bail information scheme.

Enhancing the quality of bail decisions

The Edinburgh scheme, by submitting bail information reports to the court even if no information had been verified or if the information that had been verified may not have been in the best interests of the accused, aimed to enhance the quality and breadth of information upon which the bail decision was based. The extent to which bail information reports enhanced the quality of bail decisions cannot readily be assessed, though it appears that the information contained in reports was on occasion decisive in the decision to grant bail and that fiscals, sheriffs and defence agents were generally satisfied with the credibility of the reports received. Moreover the finding that accused in both schemes for whom positive verified information may have been instrumental in facilitating their release on bail were no more likely to breach their bail orders than accused who were released in the absence of such information suggests that at the very least bail information reports were not increasing the likelihood of bail inappropriately being granted to accused who were interviewed by the schemes.

Bail accommodation

Both schemes aimed to locate accommodation for accused persons who were of no fixed address or who, for various reasons, required an alternative address. In both Glasgow and Edinburgh the accommodation function of bail staff most frequently centred around the verification of an existing address or confirmation that the accused could return to reside with relatives or friends. Although police in both cities checked out addresses offered by accused persons detained in police custody (and also when requested to do so by the courts) bail officers were better placed to verify existing addresses and locate alternative addresses for accused. Householders appeared to respond more favourably to an approach from a civilian, especially if the approach was made some time after the commission of the alleged offence and any initial anger had subsided. If an accused could not return home bail officers were able to pursue a wider range of options and were usually able to locate an alternative address without the case being continued overnight.

If accommodation could not be found on an informal basis, both schemes attempted to place accused persons within the existing range of provision. In Glasgow most accused were referred to the Hamish Allan Centre who provided overnight accommodation and a move-on address. In Edinburgh some use was made of hostels for the homeless, but most referrals were to probation hostels which provided, in addition, an element of support. Both schemes had difficulties developing accommodation resources beyond what was already available. In Glasgow this reflected, at least in part, a decision to concentrate initially on developing and establishing the bail information service. In Edinburgh the proposed landlady scheme for bailees proved difficult to establish and maintain.

A number of factors appear to have undermined the effectiveness of bail accommodation services. The existing emergency accommodation in Glasgow tended to be of a relatively poor standard but its availability nevertheless made the development of further accommodation resources less of an urgent priority. Hostels for homeless people in Edinburgh could not guarantee a bed on the basis of a telephone referral by the bail accommodation officer.

Probation hostels in both Edinburgh and Glasgow encountered difficulties in offering places to bailees: sufficient information about accused persons was often not available to enable hostels to assess the potential risk to other clients; the availability of bail beds could not be guaranteed given the priority necessarily accorded to other groups of clients; periods of residence could not

155

be determined in advance and varied from very brief to lengthy; and by virtue of their unconvicted status, bailees could not easily be managed within existing hostel rules. Few accused, in any case, were identified as requiring the degree of support that probation hostels provided.

In Edinburgh landladies proved difficult to recruit and retain. Most were reluctant to leave beds unoccupied for use by bailees. The bail accommodation officer was also reluctant to refer to landlady accommodation bailees with a history of violence, of fire-raising, of sexual offences or of mental health problems or those with problems relating to the use of alcohol or drugs.

Some accused, such as those with mental health problems or with significant alcohol or drug related difficulties, required specialist provision which was either absent or unavailable to bailees. Specialist hostels were unwilling to accept bailees without having first conducted their own assessment. Other accommodation providers, on the other hand, found it impossible to offer the levels of support that bailees with severe personal problems required.

Finally, the development of appropriate accommodation for bailees was hampered by a lack of clarity regarding the level and nature of demand and the requirements of the courts. Would the courts, for example, be prepared to allow bail even if schemes could not guarantee that the accused would continue to reside at a particular address? What level of supervision or support did court users expect if accused were provided with a bail address? Clarification of these issues was an essential prerequisite for the development of accommodation which the courts would be prepared to use and which catered for a range of bailees, especially those for whom the courts required more than simply a domicile of citation.

Bail supervision

Bail supervision was an ongoing, but unresolved, topic of discussion at advisory group meetings in Edinburgh. These meetings highlighted the different interpretations of what bail supervision should involve: the provision of support for bailees for whom this was required or the monitoring of compliance with the requirements of the bail order? Opinions also differed as to who - the bail information or accommodation officer - should be responsible for providing supervision of bailees. In practice some degree of support and supervision was being provided by the bail accommodation officer. Discussion therefore centred around whether this should be provided on a more formalised basis.

In April 1993 bail information and supervision in Scotland were brought within the 100 per cent central government funding mechanism for social work services to the criminal justice system. This has not, however, resulted in the widespread development of bail services. Some small schemes have been introduced through the re-deployment of existing resources, but bail information has not yet been prioritised by the Scottish Office and, as such, additional monies for the creation of new schemes has not been made available. Instead, the Scottish Office has funded, on a pilot basis, bail supervision as an additional component of the existing bail information and accommodation schemes. This new development, which aims to provide supervision and support to bailees, is currently the subject of independent evaluation, the findings of which are not yet available.

Bail support work is carried out in some areas of England and Wales, mainly with juvenile offenders (Cavadino and Gibson, 1993). In 1993 NACRO established a Bail Support Unit with Home Office funding to promote the development of effective support schemes in England and Wales. Mair and Lloyd (1996) have suggested that the combination of information and support may serve to allay fears about public safety, prevent further offending on bail and, where relevant, enable accused to return to court for sentencing having demonstrated a willingness to address their problems.

Implications for the development of bail services in Scotland

The experiences of the experimental schemes can be drawn upon to identify those issues which will require attention if bail information and accommodation services are to be introduced in other Scottish courts.

The planning process

The time-scale within which local authorities were required to submit proposals for the provision of bail services and implement these proposals was very tight and appears to have prevented full consideration of the various practical issues associated with the operation of a bail information and accommodation scheme. The lengthier planning process in Glasgow appears to have reduced the number of operational difficulties once the bail information service was under way. A number of factors would seem to require attention at the planning stage to ensure the subsequent smooth operation of schemes

Identifying the level and nature of demand for bail services Verified information may have an impact upon the granting of bail only if it addresses concerns which are of direct relevance to the bail decision. Confirmation of the availability of an address appeared to be most highly valued by those involved in the bail process but the extent to which accommodation is a serious impediment to the granting of bail will vary from area to area and from court to court. The extent to which existing sources of alternative accommodation are sufficient to meet the needs of bailees will likewise differ across the country and will be influenced by the needs of accused persons and the requirements of the courts.

The process of referral The manner in which cases are referred to the bail information officer requires careful consideration if the accuracy of targeting is to be maximised. Whilst targeting was not a serious problem in Edinburgh, some interviews were conducted with accused for whom bail was not subsequently opposed at the expense perhaps of others for whom bail information might have been instrumental in facilitating the granting of bail. The earlier start of the custody court in Edinburgh made it impractical for the bail information officer to wait until names were provided by the fiscal before beginning to interview accused persons who had been detained in police custody.

Organising the information and accommodation roles It was clear that the assumption by both staff in Glasgow of information and accommodation roles enabled them to respond more flexibly to the changing demands of an evolving service. The rigid division of the roles of the bail information and accommodation officers in Edinburgh prevented resources from being channelled to whichever aspect of the service required particular attention at any time. Even when the level of accommodation referrals was low, for example, the accommodation officer was unable to assist the information officer in the verification of information and provision of reports to the court. However, the experimental schemes provided services to two of Scotland's busiest courts and there appeared to be sufficient demand in both courts to justify the level of staffing which prevailed. The potential level of referrals for verified information or accommodation in smaller courts may not merit the appointment of two members of staff and in some bail services might more appropriately be provided on a part-time basis by court-based social work staff.

The inclusion of negative information Clarity is required with respect to whether or not bail information reports should contain unverified or negative information which might be detrimental to the accused. The experimental schemes adopted different positions with regard to the inclusion of such information. In Edinburgh, where an explicit aim was to improve the quality of bail decisions, it was agreed that reports would be submitted for all accused who had been interviewed. In Glasgow, unless the request for information had been initiated by the court, reports were only submitted if they contained information likely to be of advantage to the accused. Some fiscals in Glasgow were not, however, aware that only positive information would be disclosed to the court and made referrals on the understanding that all information that was verified would be made available.

In England and Wales bail schemes do not generally provide information likely to be detrimental to the accused person's chances of obtaining bail. This stance is adopted on the basis that the Crown already has sufficient information prejudicial to the granting of bail. As such, additional negative information is, at best, unnecessary and, at worst, likely to remove any chance of bail being granted to the accused. This approach has not, however, been without its difficulties, with concern being expressed by the Crown Prosecution Service and by magistrates that a scheme which provides only positive information is biased in favour of the defendant (Lloyd, 1992). This, in turn, can damage the credibility of the scheme. In its thematic inspection of bail information schemes in England and Wales, the Probation Inspectorate acknowledged the difficulties surrounding negative information and recommended that the Association of Chief Officers of Probation should provide guidance on the issue since the withholding of information could undermine trust (HM Inspectorate of Probation, 1993).

Developing relationships with others involved in the bail process

The development of effective working relationships with other court users is essential both in the planning of bail services and in their operation. Such relationships appear to have been facilitated in Glasgow by the close physical proximity of the various court users, providing an opportunity for considerable formal and informal contact with bail staff. In Edinburgh, where different agencies were located in different parts of the city there was less opportunity for regular contact of a formal or informal kind. There was, as a result, little sense of shared ownership of the Edinburgh scheme which was reflected, for instance, in the failure of court personnel and other involved in the bail process to ensure that bail information reports were circulated in court.

The advisory groups proved to be useful fora within which those involved in the bail process could review and discuss the operation of the schemes. However those represented on the advisory groups did not always, it appeared, ensure that their colleagues were fully conversant with the operation of the schemes. Both schemes therefore took additional steps to inform other agencies of their work through meetings and through the production of written information about the bail services.

The importance of staff adopting a proactive approach and maintaining contact on a regular basis with other agencies whose co-operation they require has been highlighted in other studies of innovative projects (e.g. Raynor, 1988; Warner, 1992). Although the development of effective working relationships can be time-consuming it is necessary both to ensure that the fullest possible use is made of services and to convince other key individuals and groups of the reliability and credibility of the scheme.

Ensuring that the service is visible in court

The regular presence of bail officers in court appears to have increased the profile and credibility of the Glasgow scheme. By being present in court bail staff were also in a position to ensure that reports were distributed, to ensure that they were receiving all appropriate referrals, to answer any queries from fiscals or defence agents and to offer an additional service while the court was in session thereby preventing the need for overnight remands.

Other potential developments

The experiment has served to identify other ways in which bail information services might usefully be extended.

At other points in the criminal justice process

A number of defence agents commented that they had found the information contained in bail reports useful in other circumstances such as in bail appeals, in applications for legal aid and following conviction (both when arguing in favour of bail prior to sentencing and in mitigation at sentencing).

Sheriffs had also, on occasion, requested verified information in other circumstances, such as means enquiry courts. Like defence agents, some sheriffs believed that verified information might in some cases help them reach a decision whether or not to bail convicted offenders pending the preparation of reports.

Whilst developments such as these may prove to be of limited utility there would appear to some value in exploring the extent to which verified information might make a useful contribution at other points in the criminal justice system. In England and Wales, for example, a number of probation areas have introduced Public Interest Case Assessment (PICA) schemes in which verified information about the defendant's personal circumstances is provided to the Crown Prosecution Service to help the prosecution reach a decision as to whether or not to discontinue the case on public interest grounds (Cavadino and Gibson, 1993; Mair, 1995; Mair and Lloyd, 1996).

In the event of failure to appear

It was found in the present study that bail information reports were less effective if the accused had previous convictions for failing to appear at court. In observation of court procedure it was apparent that defence agents often attempted (usually unsuccessfully) to provide acceptable explanations for an accused person's previous failure to appear. Although mechanisms already exist by which the court can be informed if an accused person has a good reason for not appearing at court, it is possible that independent verifications of the reasons for failure to appear could enable bail to be granted in more cases.

Prison based services

In England and Wales bail information schemes operating from within prisons have been shown to be effective in increasing successful applications for bail (e.g. Beamer, 1991; Lloyd, 1992; Mair, 1988; Wilkinson, undated; Williams, 1992, 1993). Such schemes generally assist accused persons in applying for bail and provide defence agents with information likely to strengthen the case for bail. While both schemes dealt with a few such cases, which had usually been referred by the defence agent, the scope for developing prison-based services in scotland has not been fully explored.

In conclusion

The Scottish experimental bail schemes have proved to be successful in facilitating the granting of bail to accused persons who would otherwise have been remanded in custody. They have done so at slightly greater financial cost but without an associated increase in the proportion of accused who allegedly breach their bail orders. However, bail information schemes alone are unlikely to impact significantly upon the numbers of accused persons remanded in custody. This is because bail decision makers - and, in particular, prosecutors - are primarily concerned with assessing the likelihood that the accused would commit further offences if released on bail. In so doing they look to factors such as criminal history and the nature and circumstances of the alleged current offence (Paterson and Whittaker, 1994; Paterson, 1996b). Bail information was most likely to be effective if it allayed fiscal's concerns about accommodation as a basis for opposing the granting of bail. Information of other kinds was occasionally of relevance to the fiscal's decision, but was of more use to sheriffs and defence agents. In this context, bail information was seen as contributing to improved decision-making by providing the court with additional factual information about the personal circumstances of the accused.

To the extent that bail decision-making is concerned with ensuring the release of accused unless there is reason to suspect that they might abuse that release, an element of prediction is inherent in bail decisions. What the present study has confirmed, however, is that such prediction is still an inexact science: many accused who might be considered the worst risks for bail were not subsequently charged with the commission of further offences during the currency of their bail order. As Mair and Lloyd (1996) have argued, attempts to develop predictors of bail abuse have met with limited success. Indeed, the application of objective methods of this type would, it has been suggested, result in bail decision-making which was unnecessarily cautious and in the remanding in custody of greater numbers of accused, many of whom would not have abused the standard conditions had they been released on bail (McIvor, 1996). Morgan (1996) has speculated that offending on bail may be an event which contains an element of randomness and is, as such, inherently difficult to predict.

Reducing the amount of delay between different stages of the criminal justice process might, on the other hand, have a direct and substantial impact upon the remand population (Henderson and Morgan, 1991). Custody time limits for summary trials and committals were phased in throughout England and Wales between 1987 and 1991 and an Inter-departmental Working Group on Pre-Trial Issues, which reported in 1990, recommended the introduction of limits on time at each stage of pre-trial proceedings for defendants released on bail. Shorter delays in the processing of cases in which bail has been granted would have a positive influence on the incidence of offending on bail. They would also, in the case of accused persons bail to hostels and other residential provision, reduce the unit costs of bail information and accommodation services.

Ultimately, however, the success of bail information and other initiatives aimed at impacting upon pre-trial decision-making will be critically influenced by the culture which exists in a particular court. Just as the outcomes of decision-making by key criminal justice agencies have been shown to differ across court areas in ways which are attributable to differences in working practices rather than differences in the types of cases involved (Paterson and Whittaker, 1994; Whittaker, 1996), so too will the effectiveness of bail information be influenced to a significant extent by the impact that it can have at various points in the bail decision-making process. This will be determined, in turn, by the ethos and working practices of the criminal justice system at the local level. The significance of the local context is reflected in the introduction of experimental bail process projects in England and Wales (Burrows et al., 1994). These projects, which have been established by the Home Office, aim to examine, in different contexts, the nature of the advice and information reaching bail decision-makers and the ways in which it flows between all of the agencies involved in the bail decision-making process; to identify possible practical improvements in the content and transmission of advice and information; and test new ideas and initiatives, assess their effects and develop best practice guidelines. The projects seek, in particular, to determine the scope for better risk assessment as a result of improvements in the sharing of information and advice between different agencies involved in the bail process. Bail process projects offer some promise as a means by which the quality of bail decision-making might be improved and the unnecessary use of custodial remands reduced.

163

References

ACOP (1990) *Fewer remanded in custody where probation services provide bail information to the Crown Prosecution Service*, Press Release, Association of Chief Officers of Probation.

Beamer, S. (1991) *A Study of HMP Holloway's Bail Unit: Users' and Staff's Perspective*, unpublished MSc. thesis, London: LSE.

Brookes, S. (1991) *The Effect of 'Re-offending' on Bail on Crime in Avon and Somerset*, Avon and Somerset Constabulary.

Burrows, J.N., Henderson, P.F. and Morgan, P.M. (1994) *Improving Bail Decisions: The Bail Process Project, Phase 1*, Research and Planning Unit Paper 90, London: Home Office.

Carvel. J. (1991) Home Office seeks places for prisoners, *The Guardian*, 20th September.

Carvel, J. (1992) Baker pledges tougher line on 'bail bandits', *The Guardian*, 26th February.

Cavadino, P. and Gibson, B. (1993) *Bail: The Law, Best Practice and the Debate*, Winchester: Waterside Press.

Daily Record (1992) *Crimewave Blamed on Bail Happy Sheriffs*, 31st January.

Ennis, J. and Nichols, T. (1991) *Offending on Bail*, Metropolitan Police Directorate of Management Report No. 16/90, London: Metropolitan Police.

Godson, D. and Mitchell, C. (1991) *Bail Information Schemes in English Magistrates' Courts*, London: Inner London Probation Service.

Greater Manchester Police (1988) *Offences Committed on Bail*, Research Paper: Greater Manchester Police.

Hedderman, C. (1991) Custody decisions for property offenders in the Crown Court, *The Howard Journal of Criminal Justice, 30*, 207-17.

Henderson, P.F. and Morgan, P.M. (1991) *Remands in Custody for Up to 28 Days: The Experiments*, Research and Planning Unit Paper 62, London: Home Office.

HM Inspectorate of Probation (1993) *Bail Information: Report of a Thematic Inspection*, London: Home Office.

164

Home Office (1981) *Estimates of Offending by those on Bail*, Statistical Bulletin No 22/81, London: HMSO.

Home Office (1988) *Report of a Working Group on the Costs of Crime*, London: Home Office Standing Conference on Crime Prevention.

Home Office (1991) *Report on the Work of the Prison Service, April 1990 - March 1991*, Cm 1724, London: HMSO.

Home Office (1993) *Criminal Statistics, England and Wales, 1992*, London: HMSO.

Jones, P. (1985) Remand decisions at Magistrates' Courts, in D. Moxon (Ed.) *Managing Criminal Justice*, London: HMSO.

Knapp, M.R.J. (1992) The principles of applied costs research, in A. Netten and J. Beecham (Eds.) *Costing Community Care: Theory and Practice*, Aldershot: Avebury.

Knapp, M.R.J. and Fenyo, A.J. (1988) Prison costs: why the variation?, *Home Office Research Bulletin, 25*, 9-13.

Knapp, M.R.J. and Netten, A. (1992) The costs of reparation and mediation, Chapter 8 of S. Warner, *Making Amends: Justice for Victims and Offenders*, Aldershot: Avebury.

Knapp, M.R.J., Robertson, E. and McIvor, G. (1992) The comparative costs of community service and custody in Scotland, *The Howard Journal of Criminal Justice, 31*, 8-30.

Lewis, H. and Mair, G. (1988) *Bail and Probation Work II: The Use of London Probation/bail Hostels for Bailees*, Home Office Research and Planning Unit Paper 46, London: HMSO.

Lothian and Borders Police (1992) *Annual Report 1991*, Edinburgh: Lothian and Borders Police.

Mair, G. (1988) *Bail and Probation Work I: The ILPS Temporary Bail Action Project*, Home Office Research and Planning Unit Paper 46, London: HMSO.

Mair, G. (1995) Developments in probation in England and Wales, in G. McIvor (Ed.) *Working with Offenders: Research Highlights in Social Work 26*, London: Jessica Kingsley.

Mair, G. and Lloyd, C. (1996) Policy and progress in the development of bail information schemes in England and Wales, in F. Paterson (Ed.) *Understanding Bail in Britain*, Edinburgh: HMSO.

McIvor, G. (1996) The impact of bail services in Scotland, in F. Paterson (Ed.) *Understanding Bail in Britain*, Edinburgh: HMSO.

Melvin, M. and Didcott, P.J. (1976) *Pre-trial Bail and Custody in the Scottish Courts*, Edinburgh: Scottish Office Central Research Unit.

Moody, S.R. (1980) *Analysis of Crown Office Bail Monitoring Exercise*, Edinburgh: Scottish Office Central Research Unit.

Morgan, P. (1992) *Offending While on Bail: A Survey of Recent Studies,* Home Office Research and Planning Unit Paper 65, London: HMSO.

Morgan, P. (1996) Bail in England and Wales: Understanding the operation of bail, in F. Paterson (Ed.) *Understanding Bail in Britain,* Edinburgh: HMSO.

NACRO (1987) *Prisoners in police cells,* NACRO Briefing, London.

NACRO (1992) *Criminal Justice Digest,* No. 73 (July), London.

NAPO (1991) Bailed to burgle, *NAPO News, 34,* October.

Netten, A. and Beecham, J. (Eds.) (1992) *Costing Community Care: Theory and Practice,* Aldershot: Avebury.

Northumbria Police (1991) *Bail and Multiple Offending: Research Project 1989-1991,* Northumbria Police.

Paterson, F. (1996a) *Understanding Bail in Britain,* Edinburgh: HMSO.

Paterson, F. (1996b) Bail in Scotland, in F. Paterson (Ed.) *Understanding Bail in Britain,* Edinburgh: HMSO.

Paterson, F. and Whittaker, C. (1994) *Operating Bail: Decision-making under the Bail (Etc) Scotland Act 1980,* Edinburgh: HMSO.

Rankin, A. and Sturz, H. (1971) The Manhattan Bail Project, in L.R. Radzinowicz & M.Z. Wolfgang (Eds.) *The Criminal in the Arms of the Law,* New York: Basic Books.

Raynor, P. (1988) *Probation as an Alternative to Custody,* Aldershot: Avebury.

Rifkind, M. (1989) Penal policy: the way ahead, *The Howard Journal of Criminal Justice, 28,* 81-90.

SACRO (1997) *Bail and Custodial Remand: Report of the Working Group,* Edinburgh: Scottish Association for the Care and Resettlement of Offenders.

Scottish Home and Health Department (1981) *Criminal Statistics Unit Bail Granting Study,* unpublished.

Scottish Legal Aid Board (1992) *Scottish Legal Aid,* Annual Report of the Sottish Legal Aid Board 1991/2, Edinburgh.

Scottish Office (1991) *Prisons in Scotland, Report for 1990-91,* Cm 1663, Edinburgh: HMSO.

Scottish Office (1992a) *Statistical Bulletin: Prisons Statistics Scotland 1990,* Edinburgh: HMSO.

Scottish Office (1992b) *Serving Scotland's Needs,* Cm 1915, Edinburgh: HMSO.

Smith v McCallum (1982) SCCR 115.

Stone, C. (1988) *Bail information for the Crown Prosecution Service,* London: Vera Institute of Justice/ACOP, London.

The Herald (1991) *Police Federation Conference,* 16th October.

Tibbitt, J. and Martin, P. (1991) *Where the Time Goes: The Allocation of 'Administration and Casework' Between Client Groups in Scottish Departments of Social Work*, Edinburgh: Scottish Office Central Research Unit.

Warner, S. (1992) *Making Amends: Justice for Victims and Offenders*, Aldershot: Avebury.

Wilkinson, J. (undated) *The Holloway Bail Unit: Review of the First Year*, unpublished report, Holloway Prison, London.

Williams, B. (1992) *Bail Information: An Evaluation of the Scheme at HM Prison Moorland*, Bradford: Horton Publishing Ltd.

Williams, B. (1993) *Bail Information Schemes in Prisons*, paper presented at the British Criminology Conference, Cardiff.

Whittaker, C. (1996) Measuring the Bail (Etc) Scotland Act 1980, in F. Paterson (Ed.) *Understanding Bail in Britain*, Edinburgh: HMSO.

Wozniak, E., Scrimgeour, P. and Nicholson, L. (1988) *Custodial Remands in Scotland*, Edinburgh: Scottish Office Central Research Unit/SHHD Criminal Statistics Unit.

Talbot, J. and Merian, P. (1991) *Where the Coal... The Aftermath of Abandonment and Cessation*. Bristol, Temple Quarry, occasional paper, in *Environment, 38*, in Water, Edinburgh's Queen Others, Central Research Unit.

Warner, K. (1997) *M.S.M. Ancestral Works On Nation, and Others*, Aldershot, Avebury.

Whittaker, J. (ed) (1992) *Coalmining Half Care: Review of the First Year*, unpublished report, Hull, City Prison, London.

Williams, H. (1992) *Risk Identification, An Evaluation of the Schemes at HM Prison, Maiden, Bristol*, Horton Publishing Ltd.

Williams, B. (1995) *BSV Committee Assists in Prisons*, paper presented at the British City Analogy Conference, Cardiff.

Whittaker, G. (1990) *Addressing the Substance Scotland Act 1980 and Persons on EBD Understanding Law in Relation to Rights*, HMSO, London.

Woolman, J., *Solicitors[?]* and Stratton, B.A. (1982) *Coal and Research in Social and Social Justice Social Research*, the Welfare Department, Clarenden.